BASED ON A TRUE STORY

# SUCCESS WITHIN US

PRINCIPLES OF BUSINESS, BELIEF, AND TRIUMPH

Ricardo Mendez

Printed in the United States of America

First Printing, 2026

www.successwithinus.com

ISBN 979-8-9945657-0-4

# TABLE OF CONTENTS

# INTRODUCTION:

This isn't your average *'Do this and you'll succeed'* book, because my story is anything but average. It's one of poverty, aggression, determination, wealth, success, failure, family, and yes, God.

If that last one scares you or makes you uncomfortable, then strap in, because this book is as much for you as it is for people who pray every morning and every night.

The best stories always are.

I didn't start out in any particular religious belief system, but I can tell you that once I learned about the reality of our Creator, universal principles, and the energy surrounding eternal laws, I found success brimming from every opportunity.

And I found opportunities everywhere I looked.

That truth is evident today in my entrepreneurial journey, which began when I chose to join the military as a medic, then took a nursing job, turned it into a physician assistant career, which led to me owning multiple businesses and ten thriving medical clinics serving thousands of people. The contrast between where I began, and where I am now, is about as stark as stepping out of a dark dungeon into broad daylight at noon on the equator.

And before you create a picture in your head of who I am and what I look like, know that I am Hispanic and speak with a thick accent to this day. While I was born in the United States, my family consisted of migrant workers that traveled wherever the jobs took us. I faced discrimination in every form, from people thinking I was less because of the tint of my skin, to teachers outright calling me stupid because English was my second language. At times I wasn't even allowed to attend public school because of my heritage. Even during my military service, I was perceived as the 'other' by soldiers who should have been my allies and comrades-in-arms.

Don't let anyone tell you these types of bigotry and intolerance are nonexistent, because they exist, and I fought through them. Even now I have people who look at me like I don't belong in my community because of my accent, as if I am still an alien in my home country.

Despite all of this, nothing was going to stop me from succeeding once I understood my own worth in the eyes of God, and the principles that allow each of us to elevate our place in this world. These are eternal truths like honesty, self-belief, respect, faith, and love. They transform every area of your life from business and family, all the way to your own inner workings.

My life is a shining example of this truth.

To understand where I ended up though, you first need to understand where I started.

Texas summers can be hot and humid, especially when you're the eighth of twelve children crammed in a house without air conditioning. When you add my Hispanic heritage and thick Spanish accent to the mix, doors did not easily open up when I knocked on them. No one expected anything of me beyond a stereotype of jail time, alcohol, and a pauper's grave after a few too many bad decisions. I was destined to follow in my father's path, which was one of violence, discrimination, and anger. The chaos of my early years practically guaranteed a negative outcome. Life was a raging ocean all around me.

One thing I had going for me though was my habit of paying close attention to the waves knocking me about. Even when I was little, life intrigued me; the smells, the sights, the sounds, all vied for my attention. Why was one man beaten for his actions while another was praised?

I wanted to learn, and observation became my primary tool.

When I had a desire to learn how to fix cars for example, I would go to the local mechanic and ask if they needed any help. Can you picture an 11-year-old sauntering into a body shop and asking if they had any jobs that needed doing? I got a lot of smiles and a few puzzled looks, but since I would work for free, generally they found a few basic tasks for me to do. Once those jobs were done, I would spend the rest of my time watching the mechanics as they worked. And it wasn't just cars either. This same pattern would continue for any skill that caught my attention.

I watched and I learned.

Home life followed a similar pattern.

My parents would get mad at my brothers and sisters, chastising them, spanking them, yelling at them. I would ask myself, *'Why is it happening?'* By observing actions and consequences I found that my siblings were not particularly obedient. They fought back at every turn whether it was the wisest thing to do or not. I realized obedience would save me from a lot of potential pain and frustration. My brother was disobedient, and he was punished. If I was obedient, my parents wouldn't need to punish me. In fact, they would be happier and then give me privileges my siblings never enjoyed.

It was a simple principle that made sense to me.

I would be obedient.

I had no idea at the time that obedience is the first law in heaven, but truth has power whether you know the *'whys'* behind it or not. I was obedient, and good things happened because of it.

One of the most transformative of those things took place when I was ten years old and has been the foundation for every aspect of my life since. It actually started three or four years earlier when my mom taught me about God and Jesus Christ. "They hear and can answer your prayers, and they understand your life," she told me.

Was that true? Even as a seven-year-old I questioned her words. If what she said was accurate, I was going to find out for myself. If God knew me, I wanted to know Him.

I certainly wanted to know if what my mom had said was true. I kind of took it as a challenge. If God existed, I wanted to meet Him, talk to Him, know Him for myself. And so, I started praying, even though I had no idea how to pray. My mother hadn't taught me how to speak to God, after all, and we weren't particularly religious to begin with. But if I was going to learn if God existed, I would need to do something, right? I started my prayer by saying, "God, I want to know you're there. What do I have to do to know that you're there?"

Nothing happened. No angels appeared. No heavenly visions opened to my view.

I wasn't one to give up though, and since I felt like such a big request on my part would require some dedication, I stuck to it. My prayers continued simply, but consistently. I just kept praying like that, on and off for almost four years.

Then one night, my father lashed out in anger as intense as the Texas heat. He screamed at my mother for reasons I don't remember; if I ever knew them in the first place. His rage spilled out of him in terrifying vulgarity.

Fear and confusion overtook me.

The sound of violence pushed against my spirit until I found myself huddled in a dark corner of the house pleading with God to save my mother, to save *me*, from this moment of hellish horror. The powerlessness of childhood crushed me as my breaths blew ragged from my mouth. There was nothing I could do or say to fix this moment of despair. I petitioned a Higher Power again and again for some miracle that would make my father stop.

And that's when I heard the voice calling my name.

It wasn't loud, but it was powerful like nothing else I had ever known. It was in my mind, but as clear as if someone spoke to me.

The voice said, "Fear not, it is I."

It wasn't my voice, and it didn't talk like I talked.

I knew it was God. My fear left instantly, replaced with concern for my mother and anger at my father.

I said, "Why is my dad like this? He treats my mom so badly." A tidal wave of resentment filled those words. If God had answered my prayers after all this time, surely, he could stop my dad from beating my mom by any means necessary.

But the response wasn't one of reflected anger; only peace and understanding.

The voice told me, "Your father had a very, very bad childhood life. His mother died when he was born. His father didn't want to take care of him, so he was sent to San Luis Potosi, Mexico with his uncle, who treated him like a slave. He never knew love. Your dad has had a hard life and has lost all hope, faith, and confidence. He doesn't trust anyone. In truth, he's jealous of your mom. That's why your dad is the way he is."

I suddenly had a completely different understanding of my dad, his violent motivations and resentments. My anger ebbed at that moment.

But this realization was only the beginning.

The experience continued for what I perceived to be hours as the Spirit of the Lord, of which I had absolutely no understanding at the time, spoke to me about Heaven and Earth, progression, purpose, and obedience.

Most importantly for my life and journey, He spoke to me about the five principles that have guided my decisions ever since. He started with honesty, telling me how we all need to learn to be honest with ourselves first, because if you're not honest with yourself, you can't be honest with anyone else. If you have no integrity, you know better than anyone that you have no integrity. Who can you trust if you can't trust yourself?

He continued from there, touching on the other four principles I mentioned earlier: self-belief, respect, faith, and love, each with the same power and authority. He touched on my future and how I should prepare for marriage, family, and my career, promising that as long as I was obedient and listened to His whisperings, I would prosper and prepare for the eternities.

Once the communication ended, I sat in that dark corner of the house as a changed young boy. I had a completely new understanding of life and myself. Even at 10 years old I knew everything had changed for me. I had been given a gift, and I needed to commit to the knowledge I have just received.

So, what does the story of 10-year-old me talking to God have to do with you and your life? Hopefully that will become clearer and clearer as we journey together in this book. I have enjoyed great success as a physician assistant, business and medical clinic owner, husband, father, and beyond because I obediently followed these ethics in the way I am going to share. They have served me incredibly well and will serve you too.

I will relate experiences big and small, highlighting choices, actions, and faith with each one. We will focus on how these doctrines impact family life, personal growth, and business success. My entire life has been framed by what I learned on that seemingly awful night over 50 years ago, and now I feel called to share them with those who will listen.

This is going to be a journey for both of us.

And if you don't believe in God? That's just fine. It's all the same energy, whether you think of goodness coming from a divine source, a universal source, or simple natural law. Apply these principles we'll be discussing, and you'll begin to see changes in your life. You'll feel a new energy within yourself, and a deeper connection with the people around you. You'll start seeing people differently, hearing them differently, loving them differently, respecting them differently. Greater opportunities will open up to you when you accept this energy.

These truths aren't exclusive to any religion; they're universal. I only ask that you bring one thing with you as we begin: faith. Not in me, and not even in God if you're not ready, but in the idea that growth is possible. That something in this book might shift the way you see your life, your choices, and your future.

I'm not here to preach or persuade. I'm here to share what I've lived, what I've learned, and why it changed everything.

So, don't be afraid. Just believe.

Those five words have carried me farther than I ever thought possible.

Let's see where they take you.

- Ricardo Mendez

# CHAPTER 1

## THE FIRST LAW: LISTEN AND DO

The August sun began to set, but the heat remained. I wiped sweat from my forehead, pitching my shovel into the dirt. Workers around me finished up for the day, tossing the last clumps of soil into piles beside the roadway ditch where soon pipelines for oil would be laid and reburied.

I was 17 years old.

"Mendez!" my foreman called. "Get over here."

Dutifully, I approached my supervisor. "Yes sir."

"What's your plan?" he asked, scraping dirt from his chin. "I heard some of the guys saying you want to go to school next month. That true?"

"Yes sir."

He shook his head. "Look, you're a good worker. You're making good money. I want to keep you on, but you can't do school and work here at the same time, man. It just don't work. You're gonna have to choose."

The foreman wasn't kidding when he said I was making good money. That summer I had averaged $450 a week as a 17-year-old in the early 70s. That's equivalent to about $1,200 today. I was doing great.

At this point I was also living on my own. At 15, I left my family to go to another town where work was more plentiful.

My parents were nowhere to be found.

I paid my own rent and bought my own food. This job with the oil company wasn't merely a part-time summer job so I could save for school clothes or have some cash to party with my friends. This was my livelihood. Mom and Dad were not going to take care of me. If I didn't have money to pay for my room, I would be out on the street. If I had to skip a meal because I was broke, then I would go hungry. It was that simple.

But I knew there was more out there for me. I was destined for greater things than digging ditches and doing the hard work while someone else made all the money. The Lord himself had told me that truth when I was 10 years old. Just because seven years had passed didn't make my heavenly communication any less vivid in my memory. I felt the pull toward a higher mortal existence, and that would require going to school, something I had done only sparingly up until that point in my life. School had never been a priority for my migrant family, and thus I had fallen well behind my peers. I couldn't even guess what my reading level was at the time. I didn't even know what a reading level was.

But I knew what God was calling me to do. I needed an education. I'll be honest though; I wasn't excited at the prospect of going to school. The experiences I'd had in elementary and junior high had not been positive. Bullying was a constant problem, and the teachers always made me feel dumb, like because I was Hispanic, I wasn't worth dealing with. It wouldn't be the easy path, but if I wanted more out of life, I would need to give more of myself and overcome my fears.

"What are you going to do?" the foreman asked. "You're leaving good money on the table, is all I'm saying."

The whispering to go to school was strong, but would I have the courage to listen to it?

## HEARING, LISTENING, DOING

"Fear not, it is I."

A simple phrase that immediately invites a sense of ease and comfort. There is a familiarity in the words that implies friendship and protection. It's like when a mother or father comforts a scared child at night with the whisper of "Don't be afraid, I'm here." Such a promise has power in all aspects of our existence, from family, to religion, to business. We excel in all three when we feel safe under the guidance of a trusted leader.

To follow that kind of leader, or to become one ourselves, we must live by five principles: honesty, self-belief, respect, faith, and love.

But before we can fully benefit from the spiritual and material blessings of those values, we must first learn to listen both spiritually and materially.

We must listen to the people around us, and the whisperings of a God who is ever ready to aid in our pursuits.

And that brings me back to "Fear not, it is I."

Those were the words the Lord spoke to me one dark evening when my father, in his vicious rage, assaulted my mother. I was a child who had no formal religious upbringing, but my desire to know whether God existed pushed me to seek Him. His message was revelatory to me and changed the direction of my life. I wasn't called to go into a lifelong ministry; rather I was called to live as an example and to be obedient in all things.

"Listen and obey," He said.

I could do that. I was naturally obedient, after all. The listening, on the other hand, would require time and practice.

Hearing is passive. Listening is creative. It calls us to act.

When the Lord speaks, it's up to us to listen.

The same thing goes for when we are interacting with employees, business leaders, our spouses and children. When someone else is speaking, they will tell us their feelings, motivations, fears and desires. When we listen, we can then find solutions to their problems or help slow the growth of misunderstandings before they become full-blown resentments. Listening is about energy; the energy of the person speaking, and the energy we bring in response.

Listening is our choice, and we must be active participants whether it's our spouse telling us how unhappy they are, or the Lord whispering how we can be of service to a suffering neighbor.

And His voice is not always as loud and forceful as we might like.

Even if heard in a whisper though, the impetus for us is to act. If we do nothing, we are hearers only. We must listen and do.

That fateful night when I was 10 years old as I hid, crying next to my bed, the voice of the Lord was unmistakable. He spoke to my mind, but they weren't my thoughts I was hearing. The voice was distinct and clear, separate from my own perceptions. He taught me principles that shaped who I am. I listened, of course, having no doubt as to who was speaking to me. The things I was taught that night were far beyond the understanding of a 10-year-old, particularly one who had no frame of reference for what was being experienced.

To give you a brief idea of what was covered (we'll get into greater details in upcoming chapters on the individual principles), I was first taught that the Earth is a similitude of the heavens. There are fathers and mothers, grandparents, kings, queens, cities, governments, rules and regulations. The same philosophies that govern life on Earth govern in heaven as well. I was taught that the term 'God' is just a title, and while there is only one God for us, our own Father in Heaven, that title of 'God' can be earned through eternal progression. The discussion flowed from the principles of chastity and marriage, to faith and the Light of Christ.

It was a download of celestial proportions!

In truly listening to this divine communication, I was committed to being obedient from then on. That was the action I was taking. When I have felt the promptings of the Lord ever since, they have always required me to act. Each time I heard his voice or felt a tug to do something at a specific moment, I didn't know what the result would be, but I trusted enough to simply act, and believe the outcome would be positive.

The wisdom behind this trust came into stark relief one evening two years later.

## THE HIDDEN GUN

I was sitting on the couch when a powerful thought came into my 12-year-old mind. I knew immediately it wasn't my own ideation, but rather something else beyond me. The words were plain and powerful.

*"Hide the gun."*

I was startled for a second because I hadn't felt such a strong spiritual prompting since the night of my original communication. I looked around to make sure I was alone.

*"Hide the gun,"* the voice repeated.

It was a straightforward enough command, but one I simply couldn't perform. I had no idea we had a gun, let alone where it was kept.

"I don't know where it is," I replied in my mind.

*"Don't worry,"* the voice answered. *"I'll show you."*

The voice guided me into the kitchen toward a door frame. I was told to grab a chair, stand on it, and reach up to the top of the frame and put my hand up there. As I did, my fingers touched cold metal. I pulled down a black revolver, loaded with bullets. My heart raced.

"What do I do with it?" I asked.

*"Hide it,"* the voice said.

And so, I did. I ran into another room and hid the gun as best I knew how, all the time wondering why it was so important an action that the Lord had seen fit to command me to do it.

I soon learned why.

About 15 minutes later, my dad came stomping into the kitchen, sweaty, face red, angry as I had ever seen him. I had no idea what was going through his mind or what had caused him to reach such a fever pitch of fury, but I knew immediately what he was looking for.

Placing his hand on the door frame, he moved it left and right searching for the pistol. A deeper scowl formed on his face as he realized the weapon was not where he had placed it.

"Where's the gun?!?" he screamed, voice echoing through the house.

My mother, who by then had entered the kitchen to do the dishes, jumped in surprise at the volume and ferocity of his yell.

"What did you do with it?" he accused, advancing on my mom. "You were the only one who knew where the gun was. What did you do with it? Tell me!"

"I haven't touched it!" Mother protested.

He slapped her and they started shrieking at each other.

I sat there at the table, shaking. Sweat beaded on my upper lip.

Their argument fizzled out quickly as my dad stormed out of the kitchen. About 40 minutes later, things had calmed down. My dad sat in a chair in the front room, seemingly having forgotten all about his outburst and the search for the gun. I decided I needed to be honest and tell him what had happened.

"Dad," I said to him, "I'm the one that took the gun and hid it."

"What did you do that for?" he asked. There was no anger in his voice, only a slight confusion as to why his 12-year-old boy would hide his pistol.

"Because God told me to," I answered.

He nodded his head and looked away for a second. I could tell the gears in his brain were grinding against each other.

"I guess I'm glad you did it," he said with a small smile. "I was going to grab it and go shoot somebody who made me mad. I was going to kill them. So, thanks for doing that, I guess."

I went and got the gun from where I had hidden it, and handed it to my dad, so I could show him respect. He looked at it and nodded again.

That was the first experience where I began to understand the correlation between hearing and acting. I had heard the voice of warning from the Spirit of the Lord, but it wasn't until I took action that I was truly listening. Because I listened, I played a role in thwarting what very well could have been a tragedy for my family, another family in our community, and possibly caused a violent rift that could have led to even more heart-breaking consequences down the road. That one act put a stop to a chain of events that no one could anticipate.

That night, God used me to protect my family—and it wouldn't be the last time.

Two years later my parents had moved us to Minnesota as migrant workers. The community was a mix of transient families and individuals seeking work. There was plenty of drinking and violence to go around.

One afternoon a massive fight broke out between my dad, my brothers, and a couple other families. Shouts turned into punches, which threatened to turn into bloodshed. I watched all of this take place from among the surrounding crowd of people, worrying what might happen if things got out of control. I rubbed my sweaty hands together, knowing nothing good would come from what was about to explode around me.

Much like the experience with the gun, I heard the spirit whisper to me again. This time it was much more of a whisper than before, as if the Lord trusted me to act without needing to shout what to do.

*"Go to the house and hide all the knives and anything pointy you can find."*

That's all I needed to hear. Obediently, I ran as fast as I could to our house, pulling all the knives from the drawers, any meat skewers, carving forks, potato peelers, you name it. I'm sure if I had found a box of toothpicks I would have hidden them too.

Moments after I had disposed of the knives, my older brother, who was 18 at the time, came rushing into the kitchen. He pulled the drawers out, spilling silverware on the floor in a tooth-grinding clatter.

"Where are the knives?!" he shouted. "Where are all the knives?"

I just sat there quietly as he rummaged around, banging things against each other in his search. His frustration soon evolved into resignation though as his hunt turned up empty. He eventually calmed down and walked out of the kitchen in defeat.

Later that night I told my dad what I had done and why. His

response was similar to what it had been two years earlier. He seemed to accept that God had told me what to do, which then kept him from making a mistake that would have destroyed more lives than just his own. What would have happened to my brothers? What would have happened to me?

I had heard the still small voice and acted.

## LISTENING FOR GOD'S WHISPERS

"So, what are you going to do?"

The voice of my foreman echoed in my brain that night after he had presented the ultimatum of choosing school or ditch digging. I had received some pretty forceful communications throughout my youth. Right now, as a 17-year-old though, I felt only a pull toward a difficult road. I could keep working and make good money up to a point, or I could go to high school like all the other kids my age and try something both uncomfortable and humbling.

I wanted to go to school, but I also wanted to earn money to pay for food and all of that. I was on my own at this point, after all. No parents were going to write me a check.

What should I do?

I waited for a grand heavenly response, but nothing came. This decision was going to have to come from me. So, what did I want? The Lord had told me to follow His path, which included greater learning. I wasn't going to learn what I needed to learn by digging ditches for oil companies. I knew that the Lord wanted me to go to school. At that point, the choice was mine.

I never heard a voice telling me which decision was right, but I understood the pull I was feeling was the prompting of the Lord; quiet, but persistent.

The next day I told my foreman I was quitting so I could attend high school. Nerves tightened my stomach, but conviction kept me steady. I would only get to where I wanted to go by being brave and taking action, even when there was no grand heavenly message to back it up.

*My high school graduation photo*

When something is right, and we know that it's right, the Lord will rarely give us instructions. But when we really need Him, His voice will be there to guide us.

One way I learned to discern the Lord's voice from my own was by comparing it to my thoughts. My voice stays in my head. His goes far deeper. It carries a feeling of peace, conviction, and urgency. When we're speaking in our own brains, we *think* the words. When the Spirit speaks to us, we *feel* the words. They move into our heart and soul, penetrating beyond the mind. When that happens there's a calmness that naturally comforts us. Whether it be peace of mind, tranquility, or chills in your body, whatever you want to call it, the sensation is the same. People often say, "I have a gut feeling," or "It just felt right." This is what I'm talking about. The feeling goes beyond logic, because if you looked at it logically, you wouldn't act at all. But because the thought brought with it a feeling of rightness, you know it came from the Holy Ghost.

Another way to gain a better understanding of the difference between personal thought and divine communication is simply through experience. The more you respond and act on those whisperings, the clearer the distinction will become. When the Lord communicates with us, He will deliver the message only until you no longer accept it. Once you deny it and choose not to act, subsequent communications will be fewer and farther between. You either accept it and do what He's telling you to do, or you decide not to do it. Once you make the decision not to listen, that's when the Holy Ghost stops communicating.

Another important aspect of spiritual communication comes down to the message itself. The Spirit will always deliver a message with purpose. Like in the example with the gun from my youth, the purpose was beyond my knowledge at the time. If I had chosen not to act, the Spirit wouldn't have said anything else to me. He wouldn't have tried to explain *why* I should go and hide the gun. The communication simply would have ended at the point I refused to listen. Once I fulfilled that first purpose though, the interaction continued.

*"Grab the chair."*

*"Put your hand on the top of the door frame."*

*"Hide the gun."*

Each of these messages came only after I had acted on the previous communication.

The purpose of that particular message had far-reaching effects. My father could have murdered someone in his anger and destroyed our family. Consequences would have spiraled from there, impacting other families and our entire community. I didn't understand the purpose until after I listened. Only then did the full picture come into view.

That's what the Lord does. He gives you the first step. He's testing you. He's testing your obedience. After that, he's giving you agency to choose if you want to act or not.

From there, it's up to you.

Just the other day a brother in my congregation, which in the Church of Jesus Christ of Latter-day Saints we refer to as a 'ward,' told me he felt prompted to invite a neighbor family to church. He heard the voice strongly but kept telling himself that he had invited them before, and they drank alcohol and hadn't been interested in returning to church activity. Even so, he followed the first rule of heaven, which is obedience, and he went and invited them. He took action, and at that moment, the family was prepared to welcome his invitation.

This spiritual nudging reaches the business side of things as well. I've had times after seeing a patient at one of my clinics where a voice whispered to me that I missed something, or that a different medication would work better for that patient. At that point, it's up to me to act. It requires courage, but every time I've done it, the outcome has been better than I'd hoped.

The more we truly listen and act, the clearer the subsequent promptings will become, until you know immediately when they are your thoughts versus those of the Holy Spirit.

## LEARNING TO LISTEN TO OTHERS

Listening extends beyond the spiritual. Indeed, in my original conversation with the Lord, He told me there was no difference between the physical and the spiritual. There is no distinction between belief and business and family. It's all spiritual.

That being the case, we must learn to listen to the people around us in order to connect and find success in any of those areas.

Remember, listening is about energy. If the person you're communicating with is in a place of anger, depression, or frustration, you must feel that energy first to discover whether they are in an emotional place needing comfort or just to talk. If you go in with the plan to simply tell them what to do, you're not listening to the energy of the situation.

Listening can lead to real change in people's lives. The primary requirement is realizing that you can't be passive. You need to pay attention to the other person's emotions and realize that sometimes asking questions isn't going to get them to open up, particularly if you aren't sincere. Why ask, "How are your kids doing?" if you don't care about the answer. Sincerity is a huge part of effective listening.

Years ago, I was called as a new bishop over our church congregation. Think of a bishop like a church pastor; an administrator and confidante that helps members of the community draw closer to Christ while also working with church finances and the overall organization of the local assembly. Right after I had been given the calling, the former bishop came up to me and told me about one of the teenage boys in the ward.

*Me during my bishop service days*

"He's disrespectful," he said. "He doesn't go to class. He's just a bad kid."

First off, that didn't sit well with me. Negative introductions, especially in a church setting, accomplish less than nothing. They taint impressions and cause us to form opinions before we've even interacted with someone.

I decided to do my own investigation, which began with a simple bishop's interview with this 16-year-old boy. It was actually the first interview I did.

The tone was open and conversational, so I got straight to the point.

"I received a report that you don't go to your classes and that you're disrespectful," I told him. "Is that true?"

"Yeah, it is," he replied.

"Why is that?"

And here is where listening became incredibly important. I needed to listen to his words without judgement and really absorb what he was saying.

"You don't see how they treat me, Bishop," this 16-year-old said with a shrug. "The classes are boring, and the teachers could care less. They don't respect me. They don't care about me. They don't listen to me."

And there it was, right there.

What this young man needed was to feel heard and loved. He didn't need a lecture about why going to class was good for him, or why he needed to respect his instructors. He needed to know he had an advocate.

So, I became that advocate.

I told him I would go to class with him and see for myself. And you know what? He was right! The classes were boring, and the teachers simply droned on and on, showing no interest in the youth.

Over the next few weeks, I talked to the teachers about this young man. I counseled with them on how to improve instruction and what the youth needed from them.

And things started to improve.

After only three months, everything had changed. This young man became one of the best youths in the ward, the exact opposite of what the old leaders had expected of him.

Truly listening to him became the key to that transformation.

While this is an example from a religious setting, the principles carry over to every aspect of life. I've had numerous experiences where employees have been on the verge of quitting, but after I sat down with them and really listened to what they had to say, I was able to salvage things and keep top-performing team members in place without any turnover. I had to listen to them, really care about what they had to say, and then take action. I would reflectively listen, repeating back what I understood from their statements, so they knew I was not only listening, but trying to understand them. As you're listening, you need confirmation. "Am I understanding what you're saying correctly?" It proves I'm hearing them.

If you're starting to understand that listening is a great deal more involved than you thought, then good.

I think we tend to go wrong, in a sense, that when we're listening, we start giving counsel. We start giving unwanted advice. That's not generally what people are seeking when they start a conversation unless they started with the sentence, "Hey! I need your advice." If that's the case, give them your thoughts as much as you want. But if they say, "I need to talk to you," they're not asking for your advice, so keep your mouth closed, your ears open, and just listen.

By practicing these listening habits, I earned the respect and love of my employees, because they felt my love and respect for them.

In family settings these principles become even more important.

Teenagers are not known for being the best communicators, which means as parents we need to listen twice as hard. Showing them the same respect we would while listening to a work colleague or ecclesiastical leader is imperative if we want our teens to open up. Part of the reason they avoid conversation is that as parents, we've only half paid attention to what they've had to say their entire lives. This isn't an indictment per se, but a truthful look at how most of us act as parents. Our little kids come up to us and want to talk about every detail of their afternoon, which can be exhausting. If we develop the habit of consistently brushing them off and implying what they have to say isn't important, our teenagers will believe we don't care what they have to say.

They will simply never talk to us.

This is natural, but not ideal.

If we all take a moment to think about it, we'll realize that we've each had experience talking to a person who obviously didn't care what we had to say. After a conversation like that, we're not likely to want to talk to that person again. Why would our kids do anything different if they feel we never listen to them?

Listening requires effort, remember? If we can take a little bit of time to really listen to our children while they're young, we'll avoid some of the pitfalls of when they transition to teenagers. We want our children to talk to us, right? If we want them to talk, *we* have to really listen.

With my children, I've always tried to show respect in conjunction with our conversations. I've spoken with my daughter before about some pretty serious subjects and immediately I wanted to talk to my wife about them to receive her counsel. Before doing that however, I asked my daughter for permission to do so. She declined, saying she only wanted to talk to me about it for now.

I respected her wishes.

What would happen if I didn't respect her desire to keep things confidential for now? She wouldn't trust me anymore. She wouldn't believe in me anymore. You start breaking that trust and whoever it is, be it a child or employee, they won't come to you again. You didn't listen to what they actually wanted. You thought you knew better. That's a great way to taint a relationship.

I treat my employees with the same respect. Sometimes they'll come to me with complaints. I simply say, "Okay, I'm listening. Am I understanding what you said? Yes? Okay. Do you want me to do something about it, or do you just want me to keep it to myself?" I ask for their permission, and if they don't want me to talk to their manager about it, I won't.

They know they can trust me.

When we listen, be it for spiritual communication or interpersonal understanding, we are taking action at every instance. We go in paying attention to the other person's energy, matching that energy with our own, reflectively listening,_and finally doing what is required of us from there.

Listening isn't passive. It's the first act of creation. Listen deeply enough, and you'll not only hear God, but you'll also begin to reflect Him in how you show up for others. It will unlock revelation, restore relationships, and give you purpose.

# CHAPTER 2

## OBEDIENCE: MENTAL ACCEPTANCE AND DISCIPLINE

Obedience is the first law of Heaven.

That means it's the first law of Earth as well.

I was told during my experience as a 10-year-old that as long as I was obedient, I would prosper in all things. "Obedience," the Lord told me, "is a spiritual principle of success."

Obedience carries a power beyond our physical understanding. When we are obedient to precepts, laws, authority figures, we are partaking in an energy that will propel us to great heights. Obedience offers us protections and blessings. It breeds trust, respect, and love.

Obedience opens the doors of opportunity!

I've mentioned before about how when I was a kid, I observed how my older brothers would get in trouble because they were disobedient. I chose to be obedient and see what happened. I found it made my parents happy, built layers of trust, and because of it I was given greater privileges and opportunities. Of all my siblings, I was the only one to be given a bicycle when I was eight years old and it had everything to do with the level of trust I had gained with my parents.

Let's use a simple example to illustrate how obedience plays a role in surprising aspects of our lives.

We're going to talk about losing weight.

This is an excellent example because it touches not only on obedience, but honesty, self-belief, and faith as well.

According to a recent Gallup News poll, 55% of adults in the United States want to lose weight. How many of them will actually achieve their goal? Less than half. Why will so many of them eventually fail?

Let's break it down.

When a person says, "I want to lose 20 pounds," are they being honest?

They may want to lose the weight, yes, but are they willing to put in the effort that losing weight requires?

The biggest key to their success will be obedience to the principles of weight loss. That means you can't drink a bunch of soda and eat nothing but Doritos if you want to lose 20 pounds. If you are disobedient to the laws that govern a healthy lifestyle, you will never achieve your goal.

It's a simple matter of obedience.

This principle extends to building a business as well. We'll go deeper into this topic in a few minutes, but the long and short of it is, if you want to be an entrepreneur and grow to become a Fortune 500 company, you need to ask yourself whether or not you're willing to be obedient to the laws that govern business. Will you put in the hours necessary to achieve that kind of success? Are you willing to learn hard lessons? Will you be humble enough to accept the fact that just because you *think* a strategy is going to work, does not mean it will work?

# OBEDIENCE AND TRUST

No discussion regarding obedience can start without bringing trust into the conversation. Many western cultures see obedience strictly in terms of submission to a person or government. In that regard, obedience takes on a negative connotation because it implies subservience to someone unworthy of that honor. We think of authority figures demanding obedience and forcing people to act against their own will or self-interest.

These are legitimate arguments.

Obedience to a person requires trust. When we are asked by an ecclesiastical leader for obedience to God's law, do we trust them as a spiritual guide? When a government passes a new regulation, do we trust it was passed in good faith for the benefit of all? When a boss asks us to be obedient to the standards of business, do we trust they will follow those same standards?

Each of us must individually grapple with the level of trust we have in all cases of obedience. For some people, no matter what law a government passes, they'll see it as an affront to their personal liberty or an act of oppression. For others, the thought of being 'obedient' to a business superior conjures images of harassment and degradation.

Obedience is a personal topic.

Even so, our individual perspectives do not negate the truth of obedience as a heavenly and earthly power. Blind obedience is not required of anyone. Having said that, we won't always have all the information we need when being asked to be obedient. In spiritual matters, God asks for our trust and promises it will pay off. Even in these circumstances we can pray for confirmation and receive feelings of comfort when we have questions about commandments or promptings. In business or military matters, we may be asked for our obedience while only knowing what individual parts of the plan we need to know. In each circumstance, trust plays a role.

But let's be truthful here. When we're asked to be obedient and we hesitate, is our reluctance because of trust issues or personal pride? Sometimes we don't want to be obedient because it makes us feel like someone else has power over us. "I should be the one giving the orders, not someone else!"

This is a dangerous mindset.

It leads us to victimize ourselves and place blame on others. In these circumstances we are seeking power only for the sake of being powerful. It causes us to tear down our peers and gossip behind our leader's backs. In those moments we prove how unworthy of obedience we are, and probably why we haven't been put in a position to give orders to other people.

Along those same lines, what happens when you are the one asking for obedience from your children, employees, constituents, or anyone else? Have you built up the trust necessary for them to follow through on what you're asking?

With high levels of trust, children will know their parents have their best interests at heart. With low levels of trust, those same children will question every rule, seeing them as unfair or inconsistent. In military settings, low trust will lead to hesitancy to fulfill orders and possibly unnecessary deaths on the battlefield. Finally, in business, when leaders have fostered a low-trust environment, passive noncompliance and overall resistance flourishes.

For me, I choose to be obedient because I have seen its power in my life. I have been obedient to laws, to leaders, to superiors, and to God. Each has brought its own blessings. It's required humility and patience, but it has been worth it. And on the opposing side, when asking for obedience in religious settings, family scenarios, or business meetings, I have tried to first engender trust and love. Without those efforts, my requests for obedience would have fallen on deaf ears.

We must ask ourselves, "Can I be trusted with the obedience of others? Will I hold myself to the same standards I am requiring of the people around me? Am I a leader who keeps my word and can be trusted to follow through?"

If the answer to any of those questions is 'No,' you have a major problem.

Only through fostering trust will we inspire obedience in others.

## OBEDIENCE AS MINDSET

Obedience is an attitude. It's who you are. You can't say, "I'm going to be obedient today and not tomorrow." You must mentally accept that obedience is a principle worth following all the time. At some point, each of us must make the decision to be obedient and simply follow through. It doesn't matter what we're doing, or how we justify our actions. If we are disobedient, we are not in the right.

Here's an example from when I worked with missionaries from our church as a member of the area mission presidency. Missionaries from the Church of Jesus Christ of Latter-day Saints tend to be young; between the ages of 18 and 21, generally. We refer to them as Elders and Sisters. They serve in pairs, or 'companionships,' where two Elders or two Sisters work together in an area for a few months before being placed in a different neighborhood with a new companion. This way Elders and Sisters get to serve with a wide array of different personality types and learn how to work well with diverse individuals.

My calling in the presidency was to council with these young men and women, help facilitate their teaching of people in the community, and make sure they were being obedient to the mission rules. When you have a couple hundred missionaries in their late teens and early 20's running around Texas doing their best to represent Jesus

Christ, you're bound to have a few who end up being less than obedient.

Such was the case one afternoon when two missionaries under my stewardship came into my office for an interview. I took them aside individually to find out what the problem was.

One of these Elders was having trouble with his companion's disobedience and didn't know how to handle the situation. The Elders had not been adhering to the curfew set for all missionaries worldwide. The simple rule states missionaries were to be in their apartments by 9:30 PM to prepare for the following day and get to bed at a decent hour. This missionary's companion was consistently pushing that curfew for the both of them (since they needed to be together at all times) with the excuse of being guided to potential church investigators.

They had recently come home at one in the morning!

This missionary didn't know what to do. He knew the mission rules but also wanted to give his companion the benefit of the doubt if the Elder thought teaching people that late into the night was something he was being called to do by the Spirit of the Lord.

An interesting quandary, right?

Not really once you break it down, which is exactly what I did for this Elder.

I asked him to explain exactly what had happened. He said, "My companion told me he felt a voice whisper to him on our way home that we should stop at the McDonalds and that a brother from the ward would have a referral for us. We were following the Spirit."

I pushed him a bit on this and he got defensive because he felt he and his companion were just doing what the Lord wanted. I replied, "Let me finish the story for you, okay? You got the referral, you went to teach the person after hours, but the person wanted nothing to do with the church. Am I right?"

The Elder lowered his head. "Yes," he replied.

"Did your being disobedient to the curfew rule lead to a good outcome?"

"No."

"That prompting couldn't have been from the Lord," I continued, "because it led to disobedience and spiritual disruption. You were being persuaded to break a rule, which the Lord is not going to ask you to do. And the fruits of that prompting weren't good—and that's how we know. Look at what happened. Immediately your companion's prompting created contention in your companionship, which eventually caused contention in your district of missionaries, which have now reached all the way to the mission presidency. And what happens when we have contention? The Spirit of the Lord isn't with us. This is how Satan disrupts the work. The fruits of his actions were all negative."

That Elder left our meeting with a new understanding of obedience and how it impacted his success as a missionary. I promised him if he was fully obedient to the rules of the mission, he and his companion would be guided toward people who wanted to learn about Jesus Christ. He took it to heart and found that promised success.

## OBEDIENCE AND BUSINESS

Just as obedience brings clarity in spiritual matters, it does the same in business. Being obedient in business means you're going to do things the right way from the start as both an employee and a leader.

This means choosing to be obedient to the principles of success.

Think back to the weight loss example we used earlier. If you choose to be disobedient to the overarching laws of health and wellness, you will not succeed in your weight loss goal.

Business is no different.

Let me give you an example from my own life.

As a young teenager, I already knew the importance of hard work and learning. I was a migrant worker until I was 15 after all, so I knew how to sweat and how it felt to come home sore after a day of real labor. I understood that if I wanted to have a better life ahead of me, I would need to learn the reason why some people succeed, and some don't, and be obedient to those ethics. It served me well.

A few years ago, a company out of California wanted to buy mine and my business partner's medical clinics. It looked like a great deal and so we moved forward in good faith. Unfortunately, on one of the calls with my partner, they accused us of bad business practices, fraud, and numerous IRS violations. The company representatives said if we signed right then under a different deal that would make us employees with salaries instead of selling as owners, they would take care of everything, otherwise they would need to report us to the authorities.

My partner called me up, terrified.

I was completely unshaken.

Why?

Because I knew we had been obedient to every law, tax code, and vetting organization in the country. Our business practices were airtight. We had no reason to worry. Still panicked about the whole situation, my partner ended up taking the deal and things fell apart after that, but I knew there was never any danger, because we had been obedient. It allowed me to make much better decisions and set me up for further success.

That's the kind of power I'm talking about when we discuss business and obedience. It's peace of mind, it's confidence, it's knowing you have nothing to hide.

And it helps you start out in a much better place from a founder's perspective.

Founding a start-up is a risky endeavor. According to Forbes, 90% of start-ups will fail within the first five years. A lot of reasons exist for why it happens, from cash flow problems to poor market development, but whatever it is, the basic truth is that most businesses will fail. That may lead some to say, "If business is so hard, I need every advantage, including lying, cheating, and stealing to get ahead. Laws are just going to hold me back!"

That may sound like a good plan on paper, but the facts don't bear it out.

A 2015 Harvard Business School study of 1,300 CEOs and CFOs found that companies with strong ethical cultures and value-based leadership teams outperformed competitors in customer satisfaction, employee retention, and overall performance.[1] Their adherence to the law, both legislative and principle-based, elevated their efforts. They started their business the right way, following the laws on the books for establishing a company, and then followed the natural laws of good business from there.

In other words, your chances of success actually *increase* when you are obedient to the laws governing business creation and operation. If the natural laws of business dictate you learn everything you can about the industry you're entering, you better do it. Research to see whether that industry is a competitive space or not, and test plans and products before you go to market.

Following those laws will lead to success.

Business is a brutal space. If you're not obedient to basic universal tenets, you're creating an energy that will push away opportunity and limit growth. If you want to become a board game manufacturer for example, you'd first need to figure out if the new techniques you want to implement are actually workable at-scale before you start buying expensive equipment. Have you spoken to

---

[1] https://hbr.org/2015/12/proof-that-positive-work-cultures-are-more-productive

experienced manufacturers in that space to find out whether your methods will be cost effective? Do you have enough capital to get you through the first few years before revenue really kicks in?

If not, you aren't being obedient to the laws of business.

And you can't simply say, "I didn't know I was supposed to do that," and think you'll avoid the heartache of failure. Obedience isn't about ignorance; it's about following the proper sequence of events in order to succeed. This means you need to learn the sequence before you start. Yes, experience plays a role, but if you learn in advance what steps are most likely to lead to success, your success will be far more likely. That's why I say you don't need to fail 10 times or 30 times before you have a profitable business like a lot of leaders say you do. You can succeed on your first try if you focus on being obedient to the laws that govern business.

That obedience must start from the very beginning. I'm talking about being obedient from the first rudimentary steps of business creation, all the way to the forging of culture and teams. Start with things like registering the company, setting up the LLC, all the actions required by your individual governing body. If you start on that obedient path and continue from there, good people will join you. They will feel the positive energy of what you're doing. They will obey your commands and follow through on their promises because they know you will do the same.

Choose to be obedient. You avoid anxiety, self-doubt, and negative consequences. It's that simple.

Obedience is the gateway. Every law, every blessing, every breakthrough, spiritual or material, flows from this principle.

# CHAPTER 3

## HONESTY: THE COST—AND REWARD—OF SPEAKING TRUTH TO YOURSELF

"You're late. We've been waiting an hour."

The words stung as if I'd been bit by a wasp.

My companion and I had rushed to the appointment as fast as we could on our bicycles, but we still ended up being depressingly late.

"I'm so sorry," I said with my thick Spanish accent. "We lost track of time earlier today and it's put us behind."

The words were true. I was being 100% honest, and yet the explanation did not make me feel any better. There I was in my early 20's, standing on the porch in my shirt and tie along with my missionary companion, explaining to a family whom we were supposed to be teaching the Gospel of Jesus Christ, about why we had not lived up to our commitment instead. The moist Spokane air made me sweaty despite the cool temperatures.

It was humbling to say the least.

We taught the family our prepared lesson, but the Spirit wasn't there. My words felt hollow in my own ears, and I can only imagine how they sounded to these people trying to learn about God and Christ. The process of teaching spiritual matters requires a great deal of trust, and we had broken that trust right off the bat before we'd even opened our mouths to preach and share.

Had this been the first or last time I had this experience, maybe it wouldn't have been so bad, but the pattern of being late had begun to exacerbate. It seemed everyday things fell by the wayside, and we would miss appointments or arrive far later than we had scheduled.

More and more we heard from people who had invited us into their homes the frustrated refrain of, "You said you'd be here at 7, but it's 7:45. We've been waiting all this time." Even worse was when one man wanting to know more about Jesus told us, "I don't think you're saying the truth because you didn't even show up yesterday. You were supposed to be here, but you lied to us."

I didn't know what to do. We were honestly trying our best, but it seemed we were falling behind every day. What more could I do?

Desperate for guidance, I turned to prayer and received an answer in a dream that changed everything. In this dream, Jesus Christ himself approached me. He asked, "Elder Mendez, what are you doing?"

"I don't understand," I replied. "What do you mean?"

"What are you doing?"

"I'm teaching the people in Spokane your gospel."

The ground suddenly shook under my feet.

"No, you're not," Christ said.

Confused, and a little defensive, I repeated, "I don't understand! I'm here to teach. That's what I'm doing."

Christ shook his head. "You're being late everywhere you go.

You are. Aren't you testifying that you have the truth of my gospel? Aren't you testifying of Me? Do you believe you have the truth of my Word?"

"I do!"

"Do you think people will believe your words," He continued, "if you told them you would arrive at a certain time and you're late, or miss the appointment entirely? Do you think they will believe you are a bringer of truth?"

In the dream, I lowered my head. He was right, of course.

"Probably not," I replied.

"Go and do as I have commanded you. Be on time. Testify the truth."

Then, He gave me a nugget of wisdom that changed my perspective on honesty and my interactions with others.

Christ finished by saying, "Whenever you are not honest, or do something you shouldn't do as a representative of Me, you allow Satan to enter the minds of the people you're trying to teach and influence them to not believe your words because your actions contradict what you're trying to teach them. They will never believe you at that point no matter how much you testify."

I realized two important truths at that moment. First, through simple calendar mismanagement, I was undermining my own honesty with the people whose lives I was trying to influence for good, and second, that by so doing I was opening the door for people to judge my actions and thus the message I was trying to share.

I awoke from the dream with a renewed focus on my time management, and the supreme importance of honesty in every aspect of my life.

# UNBREAKABLE HONESTY

Honesty is an eternal principle, which means it transcends belief. Honesty is like gravity. You can choose to believe being honest isn't going to help you in your endeavors, but that doesn't make it true. Is gravity any less real if you choose to believe it doesn't exist? Of course not!

Honesty is eternal, coupled with eternal consequences.

I had always been an honest kid growing up. As a missionary I considered myself an honest man. But my understanding of honesty shifted with that dream. Honesty was no longer simply about telling the truth as I had always thought.

Like all the principles the Lord had taught me in my youth, honesty is about energy. That energy moves through us and people can feel it regardless of their religious belief. When someone feels the energy of obedience, love, or in this case honesty, they'll want to do business with you or begin a friendship. That energy will bring them joy.

Now, as I just mentioned, honesty isn't just about truth-telling. Oh no. It's so much more than that. Honesty forges relationships that last lifetimes. On the flip side, dishonesty destroys bonds that took decades to strengthen and that seemed unbreakable. To be honest with someone you must put your trust in them; full trust, not just a cursory hope. Imagine putting all your trust in God, or in your spouse, or in an employee at your business. When you have that level of vulnerability and humility, honesty follows.

And the repercussions of that honesty are far reaching.

Here's a simple example.

I love my wife. I know I love her, and I believe she loves me. I trust her. I can tell my wife all day long that I love her, but if there is even a slight part of myself that doesn't believe it, or that is unfaithful to her, she will feel that energy and will know it isn't true.

Modern research supports what I've long believed through experience, too.

The University of California at Berkeley published a 2008 study[2] titled *The Physiology of (Dis)Honesty: Does it Impact Health?* What they found was surprising to many, but not to me. They wrote, *"Emerging research is demonstrating that dishonest acts are accompanied by distinct physiological signatures. In fact, evidence suggests that before, during, and after a dishonest act, there are physiological residues evident in the brain, body, and biology. These data suggest that dishonest acts can get under our skin and are thus embodied."*

What the study suggested is that dishonesty leaves behind physical residue that affects our actions. These actions are then perceived subconsciously by the people around us. The study further stated, *"Innocent observers of dishonesty may experience similar physiological effects. These physiological effects can have negative health outcomes."*

Similarly, a recent psychological study from the University of Rochester, focused on honesty and marriage, placed couples in a lab setting and studied how well they perceived each other's honesty. They *"examined the effects of expressing honesty, perceiving honesty, and accurately discerning honesty among romantic partners who shared so-called relationship-threatening information."* And the findings? *"We found that being more honest in expressing a desired change predicted greater personal and relationship well-being for both partners, as well as greater partner motivation to change in the moment. The same pattern emerged when the person receiving a request to change*

---

2 https://faculty.haas.berkeley.edu/dana_carney/physio.dishonesty.pdf

*perceived honesty in their partner.*"[3]

That perceived honesty affected the actions of the partner or spouse because they could feel the energy of the honest request or admission.

The energy of honest interactions is more important than the words being spoken.

# HONESTY STARTS WITH OURSELVES

If we're not honest with ourselves, how can we be honest with anyone else?

Everything starts with us individually first. If we don't love ourselves, we can't love others. If we're not honest with ourselves, we can't be honest with others. There is no greater lie than the lie we tell ourselves, after all.

So, what does it mean to be honest with oneself? Do you honestly want to lose weight, or is it just something you're saying but aren't going to follow through on? In these types of situations, we tend to know whether we're being honest with ourselves from the start. Do you want to lose weight? Yes. Do you want to do the work required? No.

Being honest with yourself requires a deep level of commitment and mental clarity. You must accept that you're willing to do whatever work is required before you set out to do something. I learned this idea from my dad early on. He told me I needed to be a 'man of my word.' "If you're a man of your word, you'll do well in life," he would say. "Nobody wants to listen to somebody that's never honest or never

---

3 https://www.rochester.edu/newscenter/the-truth-may-hurt-but-for-couples-its-worth-it-638402/

willing to do what he says he's gonna do." By understanding and accepting the rigors of whatever path we're choosing, we can honestly say to ourselves that we are willing to do the work necessary for success.

It's the same with business. We need to be obedient to the natural laws that govern business success, but we must first be honest with ourselves whether we're truly willing to put in the work necessary to achieve that success. If you're being honest with yourself, you'll then accept the need to be obedient from that point on. It's a mental decision that doesn't require a lot of mental strength, but it requires a lot of mental honesty.

I've seen this in my clinics with people trying to quit smoking. Smoking is an addiction that can be very difficult to escape. With mental acceptance and being honest with oneself, it can be done, and quickly, I've found.

It generally goes one of two ways. A person says, "I want to quit smoking." This is a 100% honest statement. They legitimately want to quit smoking. They commit to me or to another physician to give up cigarettes.

But do they commit to themselves? That's where the paths diverge.

Person #1 isn't truly honest about doing the work. They want to quit, but they don't want it to be too hard. They allow themselves to smoke a little bit in order to taper off, say half a pack a day. If you want to break a cigarette addiction, you simply must stop smoking.

That's the only way it works.

Rarely is Person #1 able to quit smoking, because they aren't being honest with themselves about their willingness to actually give up cigarettes. They come back to smoking because they never made a true commitment to themselves and weren't willing to put in the work. They believed it was too hard, and so it became an impossible task for them.

Person #2 on the other hand?

They commit to themselves first that they are willing to do the work required. They honestly believe they can do it. By accepting in their mind that they will quit smoking, they put down their cigarettes and, in my experience, nine times out of ten are able to quit then and there.

It doesn't mean it's easier for them, it's just they started out being honest with themselves regarding what they were willing to do, knowing they could do it. If they say the words, "I want to quit smoking," but lack the honest belief it's possible, they will never be able to quit. But because they are honest in that belief, they achieve what others would consider a miracle. Those are the people who never smoke again because they made a mental decision and were honest about their goals.

For me personally, this principle translates to being honest about the man I want to become. Do I want to keep learning and progressing? Yes! That means I need to be honest about accepting what that entails. That's why I watch very little television and few movies because I don't want to develop habits that will take away from my ultimate goal. I focus on other activities that will nurture my long-term objectives. I'm trying to be honest with myself and keep myself in check.

If you're thinking "This sounds hard," you're right. Honesty requires real effort, especially when being honest with ourselves. If we're constantly lying to ourselves about our beliefs, our desires, our willingness to put out effort, we are destined to fail, because we're working against ourselves from moment one.

## HONESTY IN BUSINESS

It's the same in the professional world. We know that being honest in business dealings fosters trust and long-term success. There are people who of course have built careers on dishonesty, but as our previously cited studies attest, dishonesty has deep negative impacts on relationships and personal health, so it is not a winning strategy for a fulfilled existence.

It's the energy of it, right?

Positive energy breeds more positive energy, and it's the same with negative energy. Some may use words like 'righteousness' or 'wickedness,' but at the end of the day, the energy we create around us is what manifests the outcome. If our focus is solely on greed and wealth, people will feel that. They'd perceive something isn't right and they will avoid doing business with us. The only people interested in working with us at that point will be individuals with the same self-centered focus. Their relationship with us will be solely transactional and they will only see value in our existence based on what they feel they can get from us.

The energy of this idea became very clear not too many years ago as I was trying to buy property for a building to house my newest medical clinic. I talked to the current owner and found out he already had offers much higher than I could afford. That was disappointing to me because the location was perfect for us and the community at large.

I said to him, "Look, I know I can't match the other offers you have on the table, and I'm not going to pretend I can. I'm just telling you the truth. All I'll say is that this clinic will serve a lot of people and be good for the community. They can have another McDonald's, or they can have a health clinic for their families. Just know, if we work together, I'm always going to be honest with you. I don't play games."

I then told him what we could pay, and that I understood if he couldn't accept our lower offer. It was business, and he had to look out for his own best interests.

We left the conversation there.

A couple days later he got back to me and accepted our offer, saying, "I really felt your honesty when we talked. You didn't make promises I knew you couldn't keep or try to bargain with me. You just told me the truth, and I respect the heck out of that. Let's do business."

Not only did we buy the property, but he and I became good friends to this day.

Honesty goes so much deeper than simply telling the truth. The energy of it touches people's hearts and they can feel it. They'll want to do business with you even when they can get a better deal elsewhere. And just like everywhere else, honesty in business must begin internally.

Do you honestly appreciate your employees? Do you truly care about what's going on in their lives? Is the quality of work you deliver to your customers important to you? Are your intentions positive or negative?

Ask yourself these questions truthfully. Are you surprised by the answers? If so, it's time to reevaluate whether you are being honest with yourself.

And if not, how do you change and build up your personal honesty? Let's find out together.

## FOSTERING AN HONEST MINDSET

You should know better than anyone if you're an honest person or not, right? You're the one making all these decisions in your life, after all. You're either making them with full honesty, or maybe only sometimes with honesty. Recognizing your level of honesty is easy.

Changing? That's the hard part.

Becoming an honest person, with yourself and others, requires work and faith.

Before we can choose to become a more honest person, we first need to realize why we chose to lie. Is it because we'll get a better deal on something if we lie? Do we choose to take advantage of people because we think they're naïve? Do we assume everyone else is lying and so it isn't a big deal and it's the only way we can gain an advantage?

All these reasons make sense on paper. Sometimes we *can* get a better deal if we lie about something. If we assume everyone is lying, it gives us an excuse while justifying our dishonesty at the same time.

These paths become the easy road. But the easy road rarely takes us to the best destinations. Let's take a look at the Berkley study on dishonesty again. The researchers concluded, *"When a person anticipates or engages in a moral or dishonest act, it is reflected in embodied ways such as changes in heart rate, respiration rate, and skin conductance. Changes in these physiological markers can directly impact health. For example, when we engage in small acts of honesty or virtue, our positive emotions surge, which can serve to down-regulate disorders of hyper-arousal such as anxiety. Such acts can also lead directly to health benefits such as lower blood pressure and increased longevity."*

A pretty straightforward scientific endorsement of honesty.

So, the hard road it is!

And the first step to becoming more honest and enjoying the positive fruits of that honesty is to be truthful with yourself about the level of trustworthiness you currently practice. From there, you commit to making a change.

You're not committing to me or anyone else. You're committing to yourself.

Again, honesty begins with you.

Once you're being fully honest with yourself, believing you can do it, being honest with everyone else becomes far easier. The reasons for being dishonest no longer matter because you are authentic with yourself about your desire to speak and act truthfully. It's just like with my patients trying to quit smoking. Their honest commitment made it happen. You simply mentally accept that you are an honest person, and that is what you become over time. You can't do it once and expect change. You need to be honest consistently, twice, three times, a thousand times.

Are you willing to be honest with yourself and accept that this will become a lifelong pursuit?

Whatever character we want to build, ability or skill that we want to excel in, it requires a lot of work. That's the truth of life. Big change requires commitment, honesty, and effort.

The good news is that the more you practice the principle of honesty, the easier it becomes. Before you know it, you've built a lasting habit. The fruits of your actions grow from there.

And those fruits will be very public. They always are.

Don't believe me?

How many times have you heard something along the lines of, "You're not working with (insert name here) are you? I've known them for years and they are always taking advantage of their partners. You can't trust them!" Conversely, you've probably also heard, "I love (insert name here)! They're the best. You can trust them with anything. We've worked together for 10 years, and I know they always have my back."

Imagine having a network of people all singing your praises. Naturally the doors of opportunity will open for you. Referrals will flood in because people like working with entrepreneurs and leaders they can trust.

All of this goes back to the energy of doing good. I see these as eternal philosophies that can't be denied. You can't break the law of gravity. You can only break yourself against it.

Become honest with yourself and you begin to shape your life, your reputation, and the world around you. Honesty is like gravity: invisible, inevitable, and foundational. When you ground yourself in truth, everything else aligns.

Live honestly and let that energy carry you to heights you can barely imagine.

And 20-year-old me?

He was never late again.

# CHAPTER 4

## SELF-BELIEF: QUIET STRENGTH, SOLID FOUNDATION

My pencil tapped against the desk. I glanced at the clock. Time was about up. There was no way I was going to finish the test on-time. I breathed out a frustrated breath.

"Time's up," the teacher said. "Bring up your papers and you're free to go. The reading for Chapter 4 is due tomorrow."

School had been a struggle since the day I'd started. Working in the fields and on pipeline projects had been understandable to me. High school? Not so much. I couldn't read well, couldn't speak well, and it seemed like the students took every opportunity to make sure I was aware of their disdain for my skin tone and accent. I was the stupid Mexican kid. "Go back to the fields!" "I've got some strawberries for you to pick!" They wouldn't even whisper the words.

If it had stopped there, I probably would have been fine.

But it didn't.

"I'm having a hard time with reading my English," I told the teacher as I placed my unfinished test on her desk.

"You're having trouble with a lot of things," she replied, not looking up from her papers.

"I know I could do better reading and stuff if I could get some extra help." I said the words with a mix of hope and pessimism. So far, the school system had done little to support my needs. Maybe this time would be different?

"That's *your* problem," the teacher said, eyes still glued to her papers as she marked answers wrong on tests with a red pen.

I simply nodded and shuffled toward the door.

I didn't feel very good about myself as I climbed on my bike to ride to work after school. Nobody seemed to think I had value.

Did I think I had value?

## BELIEF IN SELF

Self-belief is the quiet undercurrent to so much of life. We don't accomplish anything unless we first believe it's possible. If you don't believe you are capable of getting a promotion at your job, your actions will mirror that belief and guarantee you aren't offered the position. If on the other hand you believe you can do the job and know it is the next step in your career, your actions will mirror that belief and help deliver the promotion.

Our belief creates our reality, not the other way around. The energy we carry with us attracts other energy, positive and negative, and that energy begins with what we really believe about ourselves and our capabilities. If we believe we are unworthy of good things, the energy of that belief will repel what we claim to want. If we believe we can accomplish anything we put our mind to, that belief will propel us toward success.

This silent power of self-belief frames everything in our lives, from relationships to financial success. Here's the thing though: self-belief rarely arrives fully formed. It grows by keeping promises to yourself, finishing small things you start, choosing to act even when you're scared, and learning from each challenge instead of using it as proof you're 'not enough.'

Self-belief also eclipses whatever belief others have in you. If you know you can do something, it won't matter if other people don't believe you can do it. The same thing is true if a parent or mentor believes you can accomplish a goal. They may see your potential and greatness, but if you can't see it, you'll still fail. Self-belief is knowing you're the kind of person who will keep showing up and giving everything you have, no matter what anyone else thinks about you, for good or bad.

My entire life is one giant example of belief, from the religious to the professional. After my experience as a ten-year-old, understanding the true existence of God through divine communication, I gained a clear belief in myself and my ability to accomplish anything I needed.

If God himself answered my prayer, what could be more difficult beyond that?

I've had plenty of times other people didn't believe in me for one reason or another, but as long as I believed in myself, I could achieve anything.

During that initial conversation, as the Lord taught me these principles, I asked Him what he meant by 'self-belief,' because I didn't really understand it at that young age. He told me that you must know yourself well enough to believe that you can accomplish anything that you want to do, whether it be something small or something big. Regardless of how much knowledge you have, if you don't believe you can do something, you won't be able to do it. But even if you don't have the knowledge or the experience, if you believe you can accomplish something, you'll be able to. It's a universal, eternal law. It's an energy that comes from within.

He ended by saying, "If you cannot learn to believe in yourself, then you will have a very hard time believing in others. You cannot ask others to do something that you are not willing to do or believe you can do yourself."

It was a powerful lesson that was instantly etched into my mind.

As I've grown older, I realize that this is probably the hardest of the values to apply consistently, because doubt plays such a huge role in our existence. It's very hard, because we live in a world where we doubt so fast; so easily. We allow everything around us to shape our actions, thoughts, and decisions.

A person might say, "Hey, I feel comfortable. I think I can do it." But then somebody else comes along and says, "No, I don't think you're smart enough. I don't think you can do it." We lose that belief in ourselves. We doubt. That's why I think it's the hardest one to apply in our personal interactions, in business, and in life in general.

But it can be done!

If we *believe* it can be done.

My first test of this truth of self-belief came from an unexpected place. As a young man I had a boss who didn't think I was good enough or smart enough to even stock the shelves at my local Kroger's grocery store.

An opening for a shelf stocker came up and I applied. I was a hard worker and knew stocking shelves was not difficult. It was something I could easily do to earn money just starting out. On my first day the manager came to me and told me, "My assistant manager doesn't think you're up for this job. You're too slow. You're not cut out for this. We don't think you're going to make it. You averaged 18 boxes per hour so far. You need to stock 45 boxes per hour, minimum."

I knew I could do that many, so I got to work.

The problem was I didn't know the store yet, where the individual items needed to be placed, or the best routes to take to restock quickly. I spent a great deal of time that first day figuring out where things went on the shelves.

"You're just not good enough," the manager said at the end of my shift.

"It's only my first day," I replied.

"Doesn't matter," he said, shaking his head. "You just don't have what it takes."

One thing you need to know about me (if it hasn't been made clear already) is that if someone says I can't do something, I'm going to put every effort and ounce of energy I have into proving them wrong.

I wasn't good enough to stock shelves? I wasn't fast enough?

We'd see about that.

"How many boxes does your top stocker do per hour?" I asked.

"About 65," the manager answered. "He's been here for ten years, and nobody's been able to beat him."

"Give me three days," I said. "Three days, and if I don't produce the way you want me to, I'll walk away myself, and I'll leave the job. You don't have to fire me. I'll walk away. Do you think that's fair?"

He nodded his head. "Yeah, three days would be fair."

On my second day I concentrated on learning where all the products were, so I wasn't wasting any time. By the end of the day, I had gone up to 28 boxes per hour.

"You're doing better," the manager said. "But it's still too slow to keep you on."

"Yes, but this is my second day. I still have one more day. Give me one more day."

Day three had arrived. I pushed hard, knowing I could beat the top shelf stocker. I knew it. I had no doubt in my mind. This was an easy job after all, and I could do things way harder than this. 65 box restocks an hour was nothing because I believed I could beat it.

And I did.

At the end of my third day, I had beaten the record handily, restocking an average of 75 boxes per hour.

"Well, you did it," the manager said with a slight smile. "I guess we were wrong about you."

Darn right you were wrong!

After that, I consistently hit higher numbers than every other shelf stocker, all because I knew I could do it.

Now, you may say, "Yes, Ricardo, but stocking shelves is easy. Anyone would believe they could do that."

You may be right. But belief shapes our reality. When we trust in our ability to adapt and persevere—even when we don't have all the answers—we become unstoppable.

And it goes beyond menial tasks like stocking shelves.

What about, say, working in medicine?

## SELF-BELIEF AND BUSINESS

When I set my sights on the medical field, no one believed I could pull it off.

No one.

I didn't look or sound like a doctor, my writing skills were subpar, I had a thick accent, and my upbringing was not traditional for anyone looking to break into medicine.

But I believed I could do it. I knew I was smart enough and

hard-working enough, even if no one else did. I had made it through high school simply because I believed in myself when no one else would. If I hadn't nurtured my own self-belief from the time I was 10 years old, I would have quit school; of that I have no doubt. I knew I could graduate. If anyone bet against me, I would prove them wrong. College was brutal too. I was reading at a 9th grade level when I started, but I knew I could do it, so I kept reading and reading, slowly catching up over the next four years. The same would be true in medicine. The only person that could stop me was me.

"If I say I can do it, I can do it," I told one of my nursing instructors.

I became a nurse and worked hard to learn everything I could. I didn't have the money for medical school yet, so I would take every opportunity to gain experience. Patients would come in, and I would do their vitals as part of my job. Then I would ask a few questions like, "What are you coming in for, sir?" They would tell me, and from there I would ask them if I could check whatever was hurting them; their lungs, throat, ears, whatever. The patients would always consent. I would then listen to their breathing or look in their ears.

I was training myself.

At first, I didn't know what I was looking for of course. Over time as I would listen and look, read the charts from the doctors with their thoughts and diagnoses, I began to understand the patterns of medicine. I believed by doing this I would prepare myself for medical school. Day after day, year after year for a decade, I eventually got to the point that I was able to diagnose, give the prescription, and provide the doctors with real counsel, all that as a nurse.

And it paid huge dividends once I changed my focus from being a doctor to becoming a physician assistant. I worked with a lot of MDs obviously, but I observed how unhappy most of them were. I started talking to the doctors about why that was, and they would tell me about their long hours, lack of sleep, and high levels of stress. One day I asked one of them, "Would you recommend this profession to your son or daughter if they wanted to become a doctor?" The response was an emphatic "No!" After I asked several other doctors this same question, with the same response, I knew I had to rethink my trajectory.

Then I heard about physician assistants and how they could diagnose and do all the things I wanted to do as a doctor, plus they could own their own clinics and set their own hours. I knew that was the path for me. Add to that the fact I would only need to spend 15 months full time going through the program, and I didn't hesitate.

This was the right path for me. I believed it with all my heart. I knew that in a few years' time I would own multiple clinics. That belief was strong. And not to jump too far ahead, but I was able to achieve that goal exactly as I believed I could, simply by applying the same universal principles we're talking about now.

But I'm getting ahead of myself. Back to studying medicine.

I had been in the PA program for three months when my first challenge arrived.

One of my instructors was doing free medical work for indigenous communities and was getting overwhelmed. She thought maybe she could use some of the PA students and give them real world experience at the same time. The program director at the indigenous clinic was less than convinced.

"I don't think the PA students have enough knowledge in just their second quarter. They haven't learned much."

"I think they're smart enough and have what it takes," my instructor replied. "Give them a chance."

The director consented, but the instructor had to prove the PA students were capable. "Send me one student and I'll decide whether or not they're ready."

The next day my instructor came to me, told me this story, and about how the director didn't think the PAs could do the job. "But I think you can. Ricardo," she said. "If somebody is going to pull it off, it's going to be you."

Her belief helped to foster my own. I believed in my skills of course, but this was a big deal. Reputations were on the line. The fact that she knew I could do it helped solidify my own belief. I would have done the job either way but knowing she trusted me made everything easier.

On my first day at the indigenous site, I felt so nervous! I had never seen a patient on my own before. As a nurse, I had simply asked questions and learned, relying on the doctor to make the final assessment and assume the risk. That day it was all on me. I was representing all the PAs in my program.

Still, I knew I could do it.

The director welcomed me before sending me to see my first patient. I think she gave me the hardest case she could find. The 60-year-old man had multiple heart problems, kidney disease, diabetes, you name it. I spent 40 minutes with the patient running through everything I knew and what tests to perform. Afterwards the director took me aside to ask me some questions. It was clear from how brusque she was that she really didn't want me there. In her mind I was just an inexperienced PA with nothing to offer. She fully believed that.

But I believed something different. I believed I was a competent PA with 10 years of nursing experience that had allowed me to learn in ways no school could ever have taught me. I believed I could do anything! On top of that, my instructor believed it too.

"What's the diagnosis?" she asked with a roll of her eyes.

"60-year-old male, hypertension, diabetes, congestive heart failure..."

"Wait, stop," she said, holding up her hand. "How do you know he's suffering from congestive heart failure?"

"He's in CHF because I could hear crackles in his lungs. He's also 2+ edema. I could hear in his heart too, that..."

"Stop," the director said again. She sat back and nodded her head. "I'm very impressed. A third-year medical student would have missed the CHF diagnosis, and here you are a 2nd quarter PA, and you were able to figure it out. If the other students are as sharp as you, we may be able to bring them in and put them to work."

At that point I started feeling pretty good about myself.

My instructor was incredibly pleased, and by the time we were all in our 3rd quarter as students, the PAs started working at the indigenous site, serving the community. A lot of good has been done there in the decades since.

Imagine for a moment if I had not believed I was up to the task of working with that patient. Others can believe in you, or not, but your own belief is the deciding factor. That's what opens doors. When the situation became real, I had to believe I was up to the task.

And I was.

*When I interned into the Physician Assistant program at Stanford University*

This example proves the pivotal role self-belief plays in business. If I hadn't believed in myself, I wouldn't even have taken the chance to see the patient. I would have avoided the risk altogether. But when you believe in your own abilities, risk becomes the opener of doors. You take the chance, betting on yourself, because you believe you're a good bet.

And it translates to

employees too. I firmly believe you can take your worst employees and turn them into your best workers by believing in them. Often when you talk to underperforming team members, they have a basic belief that they aren't leaders or have nothing substantial to offer the team. This affects their performance and drive. When we as managers and owners help them change that belief by first showing how much we believe in them, their entire countenance changes, and far more quickly than you probably think.

I've shown belief in employees by giving them more responsibility and leadership roles, which in turn transformed their own belief in their abilities. Suddenly they were having a massive positive impact on the business. I believed in them enough to give them something more, and they then believed in themselves enough to outperform their previous efforts.

It's worked more times than it's failed, by a healthy margin.

## SELF-BELIEF AND PERSONAL GROWTH

Self-belief plays a dual role in personal growth and overcoming trauma. It's both the seed and the soil.

Trauma can strip away our sense of agency. But when someone begins to believe–just believe–that they have power again, healing begins.

As a bishop and leader of my religious congregation I had a woman who came in regularly for counsel. She had been sexually assaulted, and the mental anguish of that experience constantly crushed her spirit. She would enter my office crying and talking about how much it hurt inside and how depressed she was. Anxiety ruled her every action. She would do one interview after another, her victimization on full display each time. Her belief in the inability to escape what had been done to her was ruining her life. She knew she could never recover, and thus recovery was an impossibility.

But I understood if she could change that belief, light would once again fill her life. I only needed to help her see that.

During one of our interviews, she kept repeating how badly it hurt. I bluntly replied, “It doesn’t hurt.”

She was taken aback. “What did you say, Bishop?”

“I said it doesn’t hurt. The physical pain is long gone, but you’re holding onto it so tightly you can’t heal. Have you ever had a fractured bone?”

“Yes,” she nodded.

“Was the initial pain more intense than your assault?”

“Yes.”

“Why aren’t you talking about that pain then? It was worse, after all. You forgot about that pain, but you can’t forget about this pain?”

She sat silently for a moment before saying, “I’ve never thought about it that way before.”

“What happened to you was terrible,” I continued. “But it now defines your entire life. You need to forgive yourself for being a victim and start over. You haven't done that. You just stay as a victim, saying that it hurts, but all that hurt has been gone a long time now. The pain is in you because you won’t let it go. It's in the power of your mind to either get out of that victim mentality and start believing in yourself or to remain a shell of who you were. Keep going, or you stay a victim. What do you believe? That you need to be depressed for the rest of your life because of the actions of someone else? You can let it go and believe in something better. Which energy are you going to follow?”

You can say that I sounded a bit harsh, but this was someone I knew well and that I cared for deeply. I couldn’t let her waste the rest of her life without laying everything out for her. She believed that she had less value as a person after the assault than she had before, and that simply wasn't true.

She didn't deserve a life defined by someone else's cruelty.

I wanted her to believe she could let it all go and not hold herself in contempt any longer.

When dealing with trauma or seeking personal growth, our self-belief is the key factor. It can become a catalyst for change, giving us permission to step outside the familiar and expand our horizons. We can believe in our own power instead of the power other people, or circumstances, hold over us. We feel the weight of trauma and pain, but if we believe we are more powerful than both those things, true healing can begin.

We've all seen people on social media constantly lamenting how life is unfair and how the world is against them. So long as they hold that belief, it will be true. They will make it true. Their actions and worlds will create circumstances to back up that belief at every turn. They believe everyone is out to get them, and that energy will attract negativity and loss.

Luckily, we can change those beliefs. No matter how old we are or how set we are in our ways, we can change what we believe and thus change our lives. There's an amazing quote from prison warden Clifton Duffy who, in the 1940's and 50's, was well known for trying to rehabilitate the inmates in his prison. One time a critic said to him, "You should know that leopards don't change their spots!" Warden Duffy replied, "You should know I don't work with leopards. I work with men, and men change every day."

We can change! We can choose to believe that fact and see it work miracles in our lives.

Growth isn't linear. Believing in your own capacity makes you more willing to weather setbacks and view them as part of the process, not signs you should quit. You gain resilience and build emotional and spiritual strength. Your identity can shift, as personal growth often means seeing yourself as *someone who can,* and that's exactly what self-belief reinforces.

In terms of overcoming traumatic circumstances, believing in ourselves and our ability to persevere helps to restore feelings of control in our own lives.

Trauma often strips away our feelings of choice.

Self-belief restores the sense that "what I do matters," which is essential for healing.

Believing you have worth and capability allows you to see your trauma story not just as something that happened to you, but as something you've survived; something you can grow from.

Healing is built on small acts like setting boundaries, seeking help, and speaking truth. Self-belief fuels the courage to take those steps, even when they feel terrifying.

The key is that self-belief doesn't mean pretending everything is fine. It means holding onto the idea that *you are more than what happened to you* and that you have the capacity to create a different future.

In many cases, self-belief isn't something people simply 'decide' to have. It's rebuilt through repeated experiences of safety, trust, and success, often with the help of supportive relationships or therapeutic work.

When we make the decision to change our mindset and believe we are capable of more, our capacity grows. We believe in ourselves, and others will believe in us too. At that point, nothing can stop us, not past trauma, not people who would see us fail, not circumstances outside our control. We won't give up, because we believe we can accomplish anything! We will love ourselves like we never have before because we will believe we are worthy of love.

Believe in yourself. Believe in who you are. Believe that God created you for a purpose.

Believe that purpose is glorious!

# CHAPTER 5

## FAITH: NOT A STRATEGY—A WAY OF BUILDING

"I bet you 50 cents I can shoot that ant walking on the concrete over there with my BB gun!"

Not many businesses start out with a challenge like that, but even at twelve years old, I had a pretty good grasp of what would get someone's attention.

"You can't shoot an ant from this far away," the half-drunk guy said, wiping his mouth.

"I know I can!" I replied. "That's why I've got 50 cents riding on the fact that I can."

"You're on!"

And then I would shoot the ant...and earn 50 cents. I was the ant-shooting entrepreneur, not a common job description, but one that made me some pretty good money at a young age. And where had it started? Not where you probably expect.

It started with faith.

Business and faith. Most people would say they are as far apart as two things could possibly be. Others might even say they're diametrically opposed.

I would argue the opposite.

Faith is belief in what hasn't materialized yet. In business, that's called risk tolerance. But really, it's just faith in disguise. Faith steadies you during the setbacks and storms that inevitably come.

The Lord told me at ten years old that everything I see and touch is a business. The book you're reading, the couch you're sitting on, the computer you work at; every product or service is a business. I saw for the first time how deeply creation, whether spiritual or economic, is a sacred act.

I understood after my conversation with the Lord that any skill I could learn is like a business. So, if I learned all about something, I could then offer a good or service and earn money for stuff I wanted to buy, which would in turn support someone else's business. I would be creating a business that would allow me to help others create their businesses. It becomes a self-perpetuating cycle; creation that's both spiritual and practical.

That became my mentality from then on. I believed I could learn a skill, and then I had faith that skill, when coupled with effort, would yield the fruits I expected. Every job I got I would try to learn every position in that business. As was my pattern, I would simply ask if I could help others with their jobs (and normally they were very eager to show me their job). What they didn't know was that I was actually learning their skills. I would learn and observe the work they did.

And sometimes I got creative.

After watching ants crawl across the pavement in front of a group of men drinking beer one evening, I had an idea. What if I asked my dad to buy me a cheap BB gun and I practiced until I could shoot a small object or ant from far away. Then I could bet the people drinking at the bar 50 cents or a dollar that I could shoot and hit anything. I knew if I practiced, I could learn to shoot an ant (self-belief), and from there I knew that the half-inebriated patrons would pay for the chance to prove I couldn't do it (faith). I could see it all in my head, me boldly proclaiming I could shoot an ant, and the men laughing and accepting the challenge, only to lose their drinking money to a twelve-year-old boy.

I first believed in myself, and from there, I believed in the plan.

My dad bought me a $5 BB gun, and I set out to train myself to shoot ants, or anything really. I practiced hour after hour, day after day, and I became very good. I could shoot those ants every time.

Then came the hard part: walking up to the men drinking...and challenging them. I knew I could shoot and hit any ant, but would they take the bait? I wasn't going into this blind, however. I had been around drinkers my entire life. I'd studied men like this in the fields: quick to gamble, quick to overestimate themselves. I knew they'd play my game.

I could do this!

And so, I did. I walked up to one of them, made my challenge, and subsequently made 50 cents. Then I challenged the man for another 50 cents that he couldn't shoot the ant in the way I did. Oh, he wasn't going to let that challenge go unanswered! There was no way a twelve-year-old could beat him in a shooting contest!

And then, after watching them try unsuccessfully to shoot an ant, I would walk away with another 50 cents.

This quickly became a lucrative small business!

That little hustle taught me early on that success requires more than a plan; it requires faith in the unseen and action to match.

When you set out to accomplish something in business, you're telling yourself, "I want to be a businessperson, and I'm willing to submit to whatever action it takes. I'm willing to do it, and if I don't know it, I'm willing to learn it, so I can become a better businessperson." Those are the exact steps I took at twelve years old to create a successful ant-shooting business.

## FAITH AND RESULTS

Religion classes are filled with people debating the correlation between faith and works. Some people will say, "All you need is faith. You don't need works." Others will counter, "You show your faith by your works."

I fall into that second school of thought.

When you have faith, you then take action. Just like in my first business with the BB gun, you can have all the faith in the world that something will work, but until you act, that faith is meaningless. Imagine you want to start a business, but you don't actually do any work, or you don't take the time to learn the skills you know you need to learn in order to succeed. You don't check your bank account to see if you have enough money to start the business, or you don't submit the paperwork to the state to formalize your LLC.

Lack of action in any one of these areas pretty much guarantees failure.

It doesn't mean your initial faith in the idea was misguided or untrue, but your actions undermined your faith, which means you didn't get the results you believed you would get. Maybe you simply didn't want to do the work. You didn't want to sacrifice the time. If you're not willing to sacrifice and do the works, then you already know that you're not going to be a successful business owner. You're not wanting to follow those laws.

Here's another way to think about it. Sacrifice is a good word, but I think a better one is consecration. When we consecrate something, we make it sacred. Normally this is used exclusively in religious terms, but let's apply it to what we're talking about here. You can sacrifice things for your success, which is fine, but it also implies negativity. When you consecrate something though, like time, effort, or money, you are dedicating it to something bigger than yourself. If you are consecrating time to learn the skill you need, you're making that time sacred. It may take away leisure time or something else you want to do, but instead of sacrificing it, you're consecrating it.

You may think it's just semantics, but trust me, words matter. If you make something sacred in your mind, your faith will be amplified. Everything becomes more positive because you're not losing something (sacrifice), you're gifting it in exchange for something better (consecrate).

And it's the same thing on the personal and family level. Are you willing to give up all your time for your job? Is that what you want? Do you have faith you can be a good husband and father? Do you believe it's possible? If you do, then put in the work and consecrate your time accordingly.

## A PRINCIPLE OF (REAL) POWER

As we go deeper into the principle of faith, I would be remiss if I didn't discuss its power from a Godly perspective. Like with every principle in this book, faith has a prevailing energy to it. When you apply it in your life, and truly believe without doubt, miracles occur. And I'm talking about real miracles; things that seem beyond what is possible in our day-to-day life. You can interpret that energy as coming from God, or merely a universal force, but either way, the results are the same.

As a missionary teaching people about Jesus Christ in Spokane Washington, I had my fair share of rough days. We would try to bear testimony of Christ, or modern prophets, or revelation, doing everything you could to convey the truth of the message, and people would roll their eyes and tell us to move on.

It was hard and oftentimes discouraging work.

But I had faith there were people in our area that had been prepared by the Lord to hear our message. They were just waiting for us to arrive, and we could find them without knocking at a thousand different doors to meet them.

I had that level of faith, and I was willing to put in the work required to prove it.

My companion and I decided to fast, which meant going without food for the day in order to prepare ourselves spiritually. We were consecrating (not sacrificing) the food we would have eaten in order to gain greater spiritual insights. From there, we grabbed a map of the community where we taught and divided it into three separate areas.

"Now, let's pray to see which area we should focus on," I said. My companion and I bowed our heads and prayed that we would be guided to the section where a family had been prepared to hear the gospel of Jesus Christ.

I had pure faith we would receive an answer, as did my companion. Because of this, we prayed for a long time. And when I say, 'long time,' I mean for about two hours. We had faith enough in our plan to sit there praying for two hours.

"Area number 3," My companion said after we'd finished praying.

It was the same number I felt was where we should focus. We were on the right track, I knew it!

From there we divided Area # 3 into separate smaller sections, each about five blocks square. After praying a second time (for another couple hours), we both picked the same area again.

My faith was being confirmed, which pushed us forward. We both *knew* we would continue to receive answers.

"What's next?" my companion asked.

"Let's keep praying," I answered with a tired smile.

During this third prayer, I saw some clouds open and there I saw a basket full of cherries. This caught me off guard because I thought I was seeing that because I was hungry from fasting. *"Am I seeing cherries because I'm hungry?"* I asked the Lords "*Or are you telling me something.*"

The cherries disappeared and I saw clouds open up again. This time, I saw the image of a nice white house with a white picket fence and a cherry tree in the front yard. I understood that the Lord was giving me the answer I needed. I opened my eyes and looked down at the map. My vision gravitated toward one street in particular. I looked at the name.

Cherry Street.

We climbed on our bikes and headed to Cherry Street without hesitation. We had been praying for about six hours at this point, so we were ready to get out of our apartment.

As we arrived on Cherry Street, there on the corner was the white house with the picket fence and the cherry tree I had seen in my mind. I knew it the moment I saw it. We knocked on the door and Mr. Cherry answered. Yes, that was his name, Mr. Cherry, on Cherry Street. He said, "You're lucky you found me home. I usually don't come home at this time of day. Today I forgot my lunch and came to pick it up." He told us his son was a member of our church, and he wanted to hear our message. Mr. Cherry was ready to learn about the gospel of Jesus Christ.

My companion and I had shown faith, came up with a plan, executed it, put in the time and effort necessary, and we had received miraculous fruits. We had moved from one instruction (which section of our area to focus on), to the next instruction (which smaller area to focus on), to the next instruction (which street to visit), and finally, the last instruction (which house to visit). This is the pattern the Lord uses. If we had lost our belief during the process, we wouldn't have continued praying, which means we wouldn't have found that family.

I don't tell this story to prove how special I am or that I have some singular connection with God. On the contrary, I share it to prove that any of us can receive these same types of promptings or visions, if we're willing to start with faith and then do the work.

Faith breeds miracles.

That's the honest truth, but only after we consecrate our time and energy, our talents and skills, to achieving what we believe to be possible. We start by believing in ourselves, and we see the fruits of that belief when we have faith that our goal is possible. It may be starting a successful business on the first try or finding someone to teach about Jesus Christ. No matter what it is, faith is the key element that makes it a reality.

## FAITH AS A LEADERSHIP PRINCIPLE

Before we wrap up our discussion on faith, we need to delve into its power to inspire teams and individuals to perform at unseen heights.

To do that, you need to have faith in other people.

The mechanics are the same. You need to believe the person can do the job or project you give them. Faith is energy, remember. When you believe in someone, they feel that energy. You'll remember when I was training to be a physician assistant, and I was asked to go to the indigenous clinic. I believed in myself, sure, but when my instructor told me that she thought I was the best student to prove PAs could competently diagnose, my faith in myself soared. She believed in me, so I believed in myself ten-fold.

That's the type of power a good leader can have on their employees. Having faith in your staff isn't just a 'nice' leadership quality; it's catalytic. It can be the difference between someone performing at their baseline and them rising to their full potential. When a leader expresses faith in an employee, they're essentially saying: *"I see more in you than you might see in yourself."* That vote of confidence gives people permission to take risks, stretch their abilities, and grow into responsibilities that might otherwise intimidate them.

By showing faith, leaders invite employees to flourish in a safe environment. When they know mistakes won't immediately destroy trust, team members feel free to push harder and take big swings that often lead to incredible results. Faith provides that safety net. It tells people they're valued for who they are, not just what they produce. This frees them to innovate, problem-solve, and contribute authentically.

Think of faith as a mirror. People rise to reflect what they see in their leader's eyes. If a boss communicates only doubt or micromanagement, employees shrink. But when a leader shows faith – saying, "I trust your judgment, I believe in you" – people often begin believing it themselves.

So, how do we show faith in our team? Words work pretty well. You can simply tell them you have faith in them. Again, this can't be just empty words; it needs to be authentic with real energy. You must truly believe they can accomplish great things. If it's all fakery, they'll feel that energy from you and they won't believe it themselves.

Another way to show faith in people is by opening up to them. Obviously, I'm a storyteller, and I have no problem getting personal. Even so, in work environments, I always share with purpose. For me, it's a sign of trust and faith in my employees' abilities, or a way to offer new opportunities to team members who I'm looking to promote. In fact, when I share, I'll usually say something to the effect of, "You know,

I'm sharing this with you because you want me to trust you. You want greater responsibilities at the clinic. I'm sharing something personal so you can know that I believe in you. I believe that I can trust you."

I show them that I believe in them by sharing something personal. From there the conversation usually branches toward their goals and where they want to be, because they feel safe opening up about their ambitions or fear. It becomes so much easier to help them reach those goals at that point, because I know what they want.

The positive energy surrounding these types of conversations is palpable. They lead to real trust, which then opens the door for them to try new things and perform at higher levels. They know I have trust in them, that I believe in their capabilities, which in turn feeds miracles.

And that brings us to the endpoint of faith, which is pure knowledge. Once you know you can achieve something amazing, you no longer have faith.

You know it!

Once an employee understands they can perform at a higher level, they know they can do it and that becomes their new baseline. It's all a steppingstone to bigger and better things. You have faith you can start a business and earn more money. You then achieve that, and you know you can do it again with something else. You then have faith in that next endeavor, and the cycle continues.

Faith elevates us to heights we never could have reached otherwise. Be it in business, family, or your religion, faith will play an outsized role in your success, so long as you keep believing.

So have faith!

Embrace it.

You'll find yourself seeing miracles in your life.

# CHAPTER 6

## RESPECT: EARNING MORE THAN MONEY

I walked into the classroom with a big smile on my face. It was Sunday morning, the sky was clear, and I felt good to be at church after a long week of seeing medical patients. I've always loved serving in my congregation. In the Church of Jesus Christ of Latter-day Saints there are a lot of volunteer jobs, from bishop, Sunday school instructor, music leader, building clean-up coordinator, and so many more.

I've had pretty much all of these callings multiple times.

And I love it!

On this Sunday though, I was walking into the youth class to teach a lesson. I wasn't the normal instructor but was asked to fill in at the last minute, and I came in prepared to teach the gospel with enthusiasm.

As you can imagine, the teenagers in the room were not as eager to participate as I was.

My fervor can be contagious though, and soon everyone was smiling and commenting on the subject we were discussing. I had volunteers raising their hands to read scriptures, and we were going around the room quoting passages and reading from different prophets.

At this point I noticed one young man who didn't seem as enthusiastic as the other kids when I would ask for volunteers to read a scripture. I knew from past experience he did not like reading in front of his peers and doubted his reading ability. It made him anxious and embarrassed.

This isn't uncommon.

I decided it would be best to skip him without drawing attention. We moved on to the next person, and no one seemed to notice. After class, the young man told me he appreciated the fact that I remembered how he didn't like reading, and how I respected his wishes to not be forced to read aloud in front of everyone.

"I feel respected, so thanks," he said.

I hadn't gone into that situation thinking about respect, but afterwards, I spent a good deal of time pondering what the young man had said.

I had respected him by listening to his wishes and acting accordingly. A simple thing, but a powerful one.

And then I remembered my experience as a child when the Lord had taught me the principles of heaven. Respect was right up there with faith, honesty, and all the others. In fact, God taught me that He Himself shows respect to every living being by allowing each of us to make our own decisions. God has to respect the free agency of all people. It's natural law. When a person decides to do something like get drunk, or lie, God must respect that. It's their choice, and he won't stand in their way, even when the consequences will be painful. He also taught me during my original communication that the day God tries to take away the agency of man, he will cease to be God.

Agency (choice) is the key pillar of the universe and all creation. My belief is firm in that God respects our ability to choose. Individuals that break the law, whether the law of the land or the law of heaven, are then held accountable for their actions.

This truth answers the age-old question of, *'Why does God allow all these terrible things to happen?'* It's simply because he can't take away our free agency. Whenever I hear someone comment on suffering people around the world and then following it up with, "God is going to have a lot of explaining to do when I meet Him," I always think to myself, "No, *we* are going to have a lot of explaining to do to God about why *we* allowed those sorts of things to happen."

God respects us. Shouldn't we then respect ourselves and others?

## RESPECT AND SELF

In my original visitation from the Lord, I had many questions. When He was teaching me the doctrines of heaven, He mentioned respect, which was a word I heard my dad use, but I didn't really understand it.

So, I asked Him about respect and what it meant.

God said to me, "Respect is the conscious recognition of another person's inherent worth, regardless of their poverty, wealth, or societal importance. It's the same thing with the laws of the universe. Everywhere you go, there are rules, there are beliefs, there are laws. Even in heaven we have principles and commandments. You're no different here on the earth. If you learn to respect those laws and rules within yourself first, you can then give that same respect to other people. They'll know it, they'll feel it. Respect those laws, respect yourself, and go from there."

As we began this journey together at the start of this book, one of the first things we discussed was how each of these values must start first with ourselves. The same is true with respect. If someone doesn't respect themselves, their time, or their potential, they'll rarely show consistent respect toward others. Think of Respect as the public face of self-belief. When we truly value ourselves, we naturally treat others with dignity and expect the same in return.

Belief creates our reality, but belief alone is fragile. It needs protection. That's where self-respect comes in. It sets boundaries for how we treat ourselves and how we let others treat us. If we don't, burnout is the result.

But with self-respect, success becomes something you can actually carry. Accountability is a huge part of respect, and we can't show respect to ourselves unless we hold ourselves accountable for our actions. Do you follow through on your own goals even when no one knows about them? Do you keep promises to yourself with the same intensity you do for others?

You see how every principle builds one to the next? This is the perfect example.

When someone respects themselves, they no longer beg for acceptance or prove their worth in places that diminish them. That kind of clarity shapes who they let into their lives, what they tolerate, and what they walk away from. Imagine all the drunks I interacted with as a kid, or those I challenged in my ant-shooting days, if they had simply respected themselves enough to walk away from slights against their pride, instead of having to prove to everyone how smart or manly they were. What if they had respected themselves enough to cork the bottles and not wallow in self-medicated degradation?

Lives could have been eternally changed for the better!

Self-respect quiets the need to prove yourself. Your boundaries do the talking, and people listen. I'm never offered alcoholic drinks at medical conventions anymore because people know my boundaries. I respect myself enough to hold them firm. I don't budge or falter at the first challenge.

# RESPECT AS SPIRITUAL ENERGY

"I see the bugs all over my skin!" the patient said as she sat in my clinic. "Can't you see them, Doc? They're eating me. I'm scared."

Sitting three feet from the woman, I couldn't see any bugs on her skin. What I *could* see from the patient history though was that she suffered from schizophrenia and regularly hallucinated things that weren't there. The bugs simply didn't exist. Despite the unreal nature of the insects, she had picked and scratched at her skin to the point of infection. No other doctors wanted to see her.

*"She's crazy!"* they would say. *"She won't stop scratching even when I show her proof that she has no bugs on her. It drives me nuts. Almost as nuts as she is!"*

First off, judging a patient's mental state is a recipe for providing bad care. Second, just because the insects weren't real to me or anyone else, doesn't mean they weren't real to her. I decided if I wanted to help her, I needed to respect her experience. I couldn't come from a place of judgement. Instead, I sat and listened to her describe the bugs and the concern she had.

"If you say you're seeing bugs on your skin, I believe you," I said. "I respect that."

"You do?" she asked.

"I do. But do you respect me as a medical provider? Do you trust me?"

"Yeah. You're the only one I trust. No one else cares."

"Since you trust me, let me tell you this: you can see these bugs, and they are there on your arms, but they can't hurt your skin. You're protected from them. They can't harm you, so don't worry too much about them. You're scared that they're going to harm you and then you're going to get sick and die. Is that right?"

"Yes! They're going to kill me!"

"They can't hurt you," I continued. "The bugs are there. You can see them. But I can see your skin. They're not hurting you. You're safe. Don't worry too much about them. Just learn to deal with them. There are things you can't change, and this is one of them. You can't change that. But know that the insects can't hurt you, okay?"

The energy of the room changed. She stopped fidgeting. She nodded her head as if she accepted what I'd said. After that, she became a much better patient. Her skin cleared up and her personality lightened. She still saw the bugs, but they couldn't harm her anymore.

Everything changed because I respected her experience.

Now, you may say, *"Why did you say that to her? She's seeing things that aren't there. How can you respect that when you can see there are no bugs?"*

Simply telling someone they're crazy—or wrong—just because you're not experiencing the same thing as them is not the right way to communicate.

If someone says they're in pain, I need to believe them. Otherwise, how can I help solve the problem? If I told someone *I* was in pain, I'd want them to believe me.

So why is it different with someone suffering from schizophrenia? They're seeing something that isn't there—but that doesn't mean it isn't real *for them.*

I can't just say, "You're crazy. There are no bugs."

That won't help.

In terms of showing respect, we need to ask ourselves why we're doing and saying things in the way we are. Do we want to help someone, or do we want to prove ourselves right? There is a huge difference in those two intentions. One is about the other person, and one is about us. If our perceptions always have to be proven right, we'll never respect anyone who sees things differently than we do.

But when I show the patient respect and tell them I believe they are seeing what they're seeing, everything changes. They feel the energy of my respect, which helps them to trust me. From there, miracles happen, just like with the patient seeing the bugs. She stopped scratching, her skin healed, and she trusted me from then on. When I asked her to do something for her health, she would do it.

At its core, respect is a spiritual acknowledgment, a silent affirmation that something or someone holds value, regardless of their behavior or beliefs. When you respect a person's perceptions (even if they're hallucinations), you're not agreeing with the distortion. You're honoring the *person* experiencing it. Validating someone's reality isn't as important as valuing their humanity. Even when that reality is fractured, you still respect that they are a person who is suffering.

Respect is a powerful, non-verbal message: "I see your value."

And just like belief or faith, people feel respect—or the lack of it—as energy.

That's why disrespect ruins businesses and poisons relationships long before a single harsh word is spoken.

Respect has an energetic frequency. People feel seen, without being judged, when respect is present.

This resonates in every aspect of our lives, from family, to business, to religion. When we sincerely respect someone at their lowest, we echo the divine. We treat them as if they are the best version of themselves right now. When we do that, we can't help but uplift everyone around us. They will rise to meet our expectations and reflect the image we have of them in their actions.

It's not always easy, though.

I remember once years ago I was called to be the Sunday school president in my church congregation. This isn't a powerful position by any means, but it's important in that it serves to facilitate the teaching of everyone in their individual classrooms. I would work with the teachers to make sure the lessons were accurate, spiritual, and engaging.

I was also responsible for making sure church members actually went to class and didn't simply gossip in the hallways. So many members would stand in the hall talking during Sunday school, disrespecting the teacher, the other class members, and the Lord Himself. I told them I would give them three chances to show respect. The first time I would ask them nicely to go to class. The second time I would be a little more straightforward and forceful. The third time I would take them aside and interview them to find out why they were being so disrespectful to the Lord. That's the way I teach respect.

Side note: some of you who have worked in religious situations like this may think I'd be afraid of offending someone, but when it comes to people being disrespectful, I move pretty fast. I'm never on 'slow mode' worrying someone is going to get offended. I don't go that route. I'm not trying to offend anyone, but if they choose to get offended, that's on them. I've found that when I speak truth directly, without games or manipulation, people respect that. It builds trust, not offense.

Anyway, back to the people talking and gossiping in the hall during Sunday school...

I only had one person who ever pushed it to the third step...and beyond. She was the wife of the bishop, our congregation's leader.

She was a good woman, but no matter how I tried to gently encourage her to return to class, she remained firm in her preference to stay in the hallway. I found myself in a difficult position, not because I wanted to be confrontational, but because I had been asked to help preserve the spirit of our meetings. Out of respect for both her and the responsibilities I'd been given, I brought my concerns to her husband, the bishop himself. At first, nothing changed. It was a tough spot for him as well, balancing the roles of leader, husband, and peacemaker.

Eventually, we sat down for a sincere conversation. I shared how, from my perspective, trying to avoid discomfort at home might be unintentionally undermining the reverence we were striving to maintain as a congregation. To his credit, he listened with humility. He spoke with his wife, and in time, peace was restored, not just in the halls, but in the spirit of the meetings themselves.

The respect he showed me by hearing what I had to say and taking it to heart reflected his strength as a true leader.

## FROM THE TOP DOWN

Respect is often understood from the bottom up, which means we show respect to the people with authority over us. This is important of course. We're taught to show respect to police officers, political leaders, bosses, and parents. These are generally individuals with important responsibilities we don't often recognize, and they deserve our respect.

The real test of respect, however, comes from the top down, like in the example with my bishop. He was the leader, but he listened to me and was humble enough to rectify the problem I brought to him.

How do you treat the people over whom *you* have authority? How do you treat the people below you on the totem pole?

This is the true test of a leader; one too many people fail as soon as they're given authority over another person.

A great example of this is the infamous Stanford Prison Experiment[4] from 1971. In this study, students volunteered to pretend the basement of Jordan Hall was a prison. 24 students were then split into random groups of either prisoners or guards. The faculty observed but tried not to get involved. They simply wanted to see what would

---

4 https://exhibits.stanford.edu/spe

happen. The focus of the two-week experiment was to see the effects authority and powerlessness had on the students.

The study only ended up lasting *six days.*

Why?

Because the students who had been randomly assigned as guards almost immediately began treating their fellow prisoner-assigned students with increasing cruelty and dehumanizing treatment. Remember, none of these students were prison guards or criminals, and yet within six days conditions had deteriorated so much that the experiment had to be terminated. Those students who had been given power immediately lost all modicum of respect for those under their authority.

Not a great example of our human ability to hold dominion over others.

But it doesn't have to be that way! When we respect everyone at the same level, we can avoid these kinds of pitfalls.

I've seen it in my clinics again and again. I respect my employees because they're doing jobs I either don't want to do, or don't have time to do. They're making my life easier. And I respect their drive, too. I've had employees who I mentored so they could eventually leave the clinic to get a better job at another business. I remember my partner at one point saying, "You're helping our best employees get jobs somewhere else." But I told him, "No. These are good people who want to progress toward something else. Instead of fighting their ambition, I respect it. They give their best while they are with us, and we gain a reputation as a great place to grow. It's a win-win!"

I've had conversations with employees where they've shared struggles and bad habits. Respect has allowed me to understand them and help where I can.

But part of that respect is holding my own boundaries as well. If I have an employee who is consistently showing up late, I'm going to show them the respect of talking to them about it and helping them rectify the problem, but I require respect in return by them showing up on time from then on. It's a balance a lot of people choose not to reach. They think respect goes one way, but if we respect ourselves first, we'll hold to our own established standards. But, when employees feel respected, they're far more likely to take ownership of their role. They see themselves as *valued contributors*, not just task-runners.

Respect transforms a job into a calling.

Respecting people with less authority than we have isn't just a nice thing to do; it bears fruit that can be measured...especially in business. If your management style is one of disrespect or authoritarianism, you can expect that style to translate to your bottom line. Even hugely successful companies leave money on the table when they treat employees as objects instead of people. Even mild rude behavior, like offhanded comments, can reduce team performance by up to 44% in high-stakes environments.[5] Employees who experience disrespect report lower motivation, reduced collaboration, higher absenteeism, and more disengagement.

And your best employees are going to head for the exits! Good staff don't stay where they're disrespected. And when they leave, productivity drops, turnover rises, and innovation suffers. According to an MIT Sloan study, toxic culture is ten times more likely to drive attrition than pay.[6]

It goes on and on from there like a black hole.

When God told me that respect was one of the key powers of the universe, I scarcely could have understood his meaning as a 10-year-old boy. Now, over 50 years later, it's clear in every interaction I have

---

[5] https://phys.org/news/2024-08-deadly-workplace-rudeness-highlight-adverse.html?utm_source=chatgpt.com

[6] https://sloanreview.mit.edu/article/toxic-culture-is-driving-the-great-resignation/?utm_source=chatgpt.com

with employees, colleagues, community leaders, and strangers on the street. How you treat those 'under' you says more about your leadership than how you deal with those 'above' you. Respecting people who have nothing to offer you mirrors your values in action. It's how integrity shows up in human form.

And if you don't believe me, look to the words of Jesus Christ himself as he said in Matthew 5:47: *"And if ye salute your brethren only, what do ye more than others? Do not even the publicans so?"*

This verse comes from Jesus's Sermon on the Mount as part of his teaching on loving your enemies. The broader context of the passage is much more than this though. It's a call to go beyond the minimum requirement of the law and to love all people, not just those who can do something for you or who are 'more important' than you. Anyone can show respect to a governor, president, or someone with power, but it's the true leader that shows respect to the people at the bottom of society's hierarchy with equal measure.

A great example of this takes us back to my church calling as the Sunday School president.

Before I could perform my duties–and get people out of the hallways during class–I needed to be set apart with the authority for this calling. I also had to choose two counselors to work beside me.

I wasn't sure who to pick. So, I started to get to know the people of the congregation.

As I did, I noticed a brother who never wore a white shirt and tie. That's not unusual for new converts. But this brother had been a member for over 30 years.

I asked the bishop about him, and he said, "Oh, he's just one of those guys that has to be shown in the scriptures where something is commanded, otherwise he won't do it. Nothing in the Bible or Doctrine and Covenants says you need to wear a white shirt and tie, so he doesn't wear one. He's not particularly obedient or respectful, either."

It's true, there's nothing in scripture saying you need to dress up for church, but when prophets say things like, *Worship the Lord in holy attire*, I interpret that as meaning you worship God in your best clothing, whatever that clothing may be. For some people it may be a t-shirt, but here in the United States it usually translates to a shirt and tie because we have easy access to those types of clothing. If a brother had been a member for 30 years and the only reason he wouldn't wear a shirt and tie was because he wasn't explicitly commanded to do so, I saw that as disrespectful, just as the bishop had.

But I also felt in my heart that this man should be one of my counselors in the Sunday School presidency.

An interesting quandary.

The bishop was hesitant but trusted my instincts. So, I took this brother aside. The spirit whispered to me what I should say, and I followed His lead.

"Brother, I've been called as the Sunday School President," I told this man with a smile.

"Yeah, I heard," he nodded.

"Brother, the Lord wants for you to be called to be a counselor in the Sunday School presidency, but there's only one condition and one requirement."

"What's that?" he asked.

"You need to wear a white shirt and tie every Sunday to fulfill your calling. If you accept the calling, that is the requirement. You need to respect the Lord, and to respect yourself."

He sat there for a moment, eyes blinking. I wasn't sure how he would respond, so I sat silently as well, letting him ponder.

"I'll do it," he said finally. "I'll be your counselor, and I'll start wearing a white shirt and tie every Sunday."

"Excellent!" We stood and shook hands. I now had my first

counselor.

A few weeks later this brother came to me and told me he appreciated my having called him to this position.

"Brother Mendez," he beamed, "I've been praying for years and years and years that I could one day have a calling and a responsibility, and I've never had one. Thank you for this."

I shook my head. "Don't thank me. The calling came from the Lord. He had one requirement, and you met it head-on, with respect for God."

"I did! And you respected me, Brother Mendez. Thank you for that."

This brother changed almost overnight. Members of the congregation were shocked at how engaged he became. His countenance shifted completely. He no longer fought everything or asked for proof of what someone was teaching. He felt the Spirit and began to be guided by it.

I had respected him enough to raise the standard of his conduct. He had then respected his God and himself by following the simplest of requirements. That respect changed everything. I could have thought, "This guy is a jerk and isn't worthy of my respect. He deserves to be treated like the resentful man he is." And had I done that, he may have waited years for another opportunity for someone to show him the respect of offering him a chance and a challenge.

And 30 years later, he's still wearing a white shirt and tie every Sunday.

If we only show respect to those with authority over us, we'll never reach the heights we want to reach in our businesses, our families, or our personal endeavors. We'll find ourselves in the unenviable position of being feared but not respected.

Fear and disrespect may get results, but they're fleeting and empty.

Respect on the other hand builds relationships that expand into the eternities.

Such is the power of universal principles.

# CHAPTER 7

## LOVE: YES, LOVE BELONGS IN BUSINESS

"I love you!"

Those three words have a great deal of power. They impact our lives in ways that are hard to comprehend at the time. They set us on new paths and alter trajectories we thought set in stone.

But we also have a deep misunderstanding of the word 'love' in our society and in our world at large. Love is more than mere romantic attachment. It's a deeper connection that links all of us together.

"There are three types of love, Ricardo," the Lord said to me during my original communication. "There is mental love, physical love, and spiritual love. Let me teach you about each of them so you can discern for yourself which love you are feeling throughout your life. Physical love is the power of attraction. When you see someone you find lovely or beautiful, you are attracted to them physically. This could also be described as Romantic Love. Your heart beats faster when you see them and you want to be close to them.

"Mental Love is beyond the physical; it is the realization that you love another person regardless of any physical attraction. You love them based on who they are and how they interact with you. This is a comprehension that you love your spouse, your friends, neighbors, even your enemies.

"The final and deepest love is Spiritual Love. You fall in love with the soul of that person, the spirit of that person. And then, no matter what changes about that individual over time, you still love them. Mental love will change over time as the person you love changes. Physical love is also going to change because the physical body is going to change. But the spiritual love will always be there. It is eternal. You can grow to spiritually love all men and women, for they are your brothers and sisters in your eternal family."

He could have ended it there and it would have been enough to keep my mind spinning for days, but God wasn't finished yet. He needed to pass along the most important part of love, just as he had the other principles.

"But remember, Ricardo," He said, "like honesty and obedience, and the other values I have taught you, love begins first with the self. You must love yourself before you can truly love anyone else. That is how you learn what love is, by loving yourself and understanding your true worth. If you know you are worthy of My love, and your own love, you can give real love to others. They will feel that real love because the energy will touch their hearts. Love yourself and then love others."

You can imagine how this hit my tender heart that night. My mom and dad were fighting after all. Shouts echoed through the small house. Things had turned violent. I was scared enough to kneel before God and plead for help. Now I was being taught about love in its purest form.

In the years since this experience, my understanding of love, within the Lord's context, has expanded. This is where, *'Do unto others what you would have done unto you'* comes from. When we love ourselves and want the best for us, we then immediately want the best for other people.

That means if you own a business making a certain product, you're going to naturally want to make sure that product is safe for the people who buy it, because *you* wouldn't want to be sold a faulty product that puts you or your family in danger. The money is secondary because you love those people and want the best for them even though you've never met them. It doesn't matter if that person is your spouse, child, grandparent, or a complete stranger. They are a child of God, and you want the same for them as you would want for yourself.

## THE FICTIONS OF ROMANTIC LOVE

In our culture, love is seen almost exclusively through a romance lens. A man and woman fall in love at first sight, and all is right with the world. They live *'happily ever after,'* as it were. Other forms of love, both platonic and familial, take a back seat to this idea of romantic love.

The problem with this is that we forget that real love grows over time. Physical love is merely a base for the growth of the other two. So many relationships fail after a few years because their love never makes it beyond the physical phase.

Neuroscientists have found that the first stage of physical love, often known as the infatuation stage, only lasts between 18 months and three years. This doesn't mean love only lasts that long, but the biological side has an expiration date, and if other, deeper forms of love aren't established during that time, the romantic relationship will fizzle and fade.

Plus, many relationships don't start from that *'Love at first sight'* myth. Nor does physical love need to be the first component in a romantic affair.

I know this firsthand.

Let me tell you about how my wife and I met, to illustrate this point.

From the time I was 10 years old, I wanted to have a relationship based on spiritual love, not physical. Yes, physical love would be very important, and is important in any successful marriage, but I wanted a strong spiritual foundation first, because I knew that was the true bedrock of a lasting eternal marriage.

So, I said to myself at that young age, “The woman that I marry is gonna be one that doesn't know me, and when I ask her to marry me, she’ll say, ‘yes.’ That's gonna be my wife!”

You can say that idea was simply the naivete of a young boy, but at this point you should know me well enough that if I say something, I’m going to do it. And this was no different.

I met a woman after my missionary service and felt drawn to her spiritually. I knew in my heart from the moment we met that we would make a good spiritual match. I fasted and prayed for four days. On my third day of fasting. The spirit informed me that when she was 23 years old, she was sexually assaulted. The lord told me she is scared of men and marriage. She will need to decide on her own. The lord said, “Don’t worry if she chooses not to marry you. I will bless you with a good wife.”

After the fast, I told her my intent. She said, “Aren't you doing it backwards? Shouldn’t I be your girlfriend first and then be your wife.”

“I am looking for a wife, not a girlfriend.” I continued and said, “I know that when you were 23 years old something happened to you that changed your whole perspective of love and marriage.”

She responded, “How did you know that?”

I told her, “The Spirit revealed it to me. I love you for who you are. It doesn’t matter what happened to you. I would love for you to be my wife."

After this conversation, she told me she needed to think about it. I then told her I would give her a year to decide.

I was willing to wait for what I knew to be right.

I had only talked to her three times. She didn't know me at all. It was up to her to decide. She had her free agency to choose. After about a month, I was instructed by the spirit to join the military. I informed her of my decision and that I would call her once a month to check on her.

"I will not pressure you to make a decision to marry me," I said.

I was sent to San Francisco, California, for my military post duty. As I was driving into San Francisco valley I heard the Lord's voice tell me, "She will not be marrying you. Don't worry, I will bless you with a good wife."

Six months later, I found the woman who would be my bride.

We met through our church congregation. I was looking for a Spanish unit in the church after having arrived in San Francisco. I found one about 25 minutes to the south in San Bruno. When I arrived, the ward mission leader met me, and I introduced myself. He then pointed to a woman in the front row and told me it was her first time too. I went over to her and introduced myself but didn't tell her it was also my first time in the ward.

"I'm Leticia," she said, shaking my hand.

"Welcome to the ward," I said, rubbing my freshly shaved head from basic training. "I hope you feel welcome, and you know we're happy that you are here today."

That was it. I sat somewhere else in the congregation for the meeting, and the following week I found a branch of the church closer to where I was living that was also a Spanish congregation, and I went there after that.

End of story!

Except it wasn't.

Almost immediately I was called to the branch presidency and started welcoming visitors and new members every Sunday. Well, about a month after I started attending, in walks Leticia. She had learned about this congregation, and it was closer to where she lived too.

Lucky me! Plus, I had hair now, so that would surely work in my favor.

I confidently walked over and asked if she remembered me, which she did.

"Tomorrow is Labor Day," I told her, "and we're having a branch activity. You're welcome to join us."

"Oh, I'd love to, but I can't. I don't have a ride."

We could fix that. "I am picking someone else up," I said. "I could come by and grab you."

"That would be great!"

So, the next day I went and picked her up. We talked while I drove to grab the other person I had promised to take to the activity. We talked while we waited for the event to begin. We talked until it was time for me to do my duties as a branch representative.

I went around during the activity talking to each individual and family. Leticia was the last person I talked to after I had mingled for a while. The subject of boyfriends and girlfriends came up as we chatted. I told her, "I will be honest with you. There is a young lady in Houston whom I promised I would marry. I am not looking for anyone right now."

When I finished saying the words, the Lord gave me a glimpse into her thoughts. I could hear her voice in my mind saying, "Es el! Es el!" which in English means, "It's him! It's him!"

I felt bold to tell her what the Spirit had whispered. "I know what you're thinking," I said.

"What is that?"

You're saying in your mind "It's him. It's him."

Her eyes went wide. "How do you know that?"

"The Spirit let me hear it."

I then told her again about the other girl who I was waiting for and how I had given her a year to decide to marry me, but it had only been six months.

Then, words came out of my mouth that I didn't intend to say. It was as if the Spirit was suddenly speaking for me.

"If the other girl says 'no,' I would love for you to be my wife."

What? Had I said that? I think that the Spirit spoke for me because I wouldn't have said those words myself. As bold as I am as a person, I knew it wasn't me that said those words.

I repeated in my head, *"Did I just say that? Now I must keep my word."*

She quickly said, "I accept," with a smile.

I repeated, "Do you understand that I have given my word to another girl in Houston and she has 6 months to decide if we will be married? Are you willing to accept the fact that if she says yes, I will marry her? Are you willing to wait 6 months not knowing what will happen?"

"I am willing to wait," she nodded.

While I was driving home, I heard the voice tell me, "It will be very hard for Leticia to wait for 6 months."

I wasn't sure what to do. I knew the other girl in Houston was not going to marry me. The pride was getting in the way though, because I had given her my word, and she still had six months to think about it. I did not want to break my promise. I wanted to hear it directly from her mouth that she wasn't going to marry me.

It was the next day when I was scheduled to call the girl from Houston. The conversation started as usual, "How are you doing?" and so on.

"I feel that I must give you an answer now," she said as the conversation went quiet for a moment.

"You still have 6 months to decide," I replied. "I'm not going to push you."

"I know, but I feel I must tell you now. I have not felt that I should marry you in the 6 months since you asked me. I doubt it will change in the next 6 months. I will not be marrying you. I wish you the best of luck. I know you will find a wonderful wife. You are a good person."

And that was it.

I don't think a man has ever been so happy to have a woman tell him she didn't want to marry him as I was at that moment.

I called Leticia with excitement. "The girl from Houston just told me she will not be marrying me. Will you marry me?"

She said "yes," with excitement. "I knew without a doubt that she was going to say no. I just knew it."

"Are you ready to get married tomorrow?" I asked.

I was ready!

She was too...but had one request.

"All of my family is in Mexico," she replied. "I want to send invitations to them before we get married. I know they can't come, but I want them to know about it first."

So, we went and priced out invitations and found out how long they would take to print and get mailed. We settled on December 3rd to get married, which was a few months away. And that was the day we were sealed together for time and all eternity.

And we've been married ever since. Now we have children and grandchildren of our own.

You can see that this clearly wasn't a *'love at first sight'* situation. Yes, there was attraction, but it wasn't infatuation.

When I asked her to marry me on that Labor Day afternoon, I wasn't in love with her physically or mentally. I hadn't fantasized about getting married to her or even kissing her yet. We were two young people having a great conversation. But obviously the spiritual connection was deeper and more powerful than either of us realized.

After I asked her to marry me, suddenly a spiritual love blossomed. I knew we were supposed to be together on a spiritual level. From there, I gained a mental love; I knew that I loved her. Finally, I loved her physically, wanting to be close to her and be one with her.

The whole thing was quite backwards from what we think of as a traditional love story. It wasn't physical, mental, and spiritual, but spiritual, mental, then physical. In fact, we only saw each other once a week up until the time we got married because I wanted to be chaste before my marriage, and she wanted the same, so we could be sealed for time and all eternity in the temple, as per our religious beliefs.

And from there, our love continued to grow and blossom year after year. Yes, we had the same struggles and disputes that plague any marriage, but our foundation from the very first moment was spiritual, so I knew we could make it through whatever the world threw at us.

Your own relationships don't need to follow the standard physical, mental, spiritual trajectory of romance. You can start backwards and succeed just fine.

Many cultures to this day still practice the tradition of arranged marriages, where the parents get together and choose their child's spouse. And yet, these marriages too succeed and grow into loving and fulfilling relationships without the standard infatuation coming first. They become infatuated with each other over time, and that infatuation can then last decades, or even the rest of their lives.

Now *that* is a beautiful testament to spiritual love. And it transcends romance. You can spiritually love the people around you and build friendships that last into the eternities.

Spiritual love doesn't have to equal romance.

But when it does, you can build a marriage that becomes something people strive to emulate.

## LOVING YOUR ENEMIES

This is a hard one. It's easy to spout from the pulpit about loving your enemies, but when you get down to it, to love someone that's hurt you, there's nothing easy about that. Especially when it's an enemy that didn't hurt you directly, but instead hurt someone you love.

Like one of your children.

What do you do then?

I'm speaking from experience here. This isn't going to be a

philosophical discussion about war and battle and turning the other cheek against racism like what I've faced in my life. No, this is about watching someone you love, someone you were called to protect, be hurt by a person you trusted. This is real, and the pain is real.

But the peace is real too. That I promise.

When my daughter was 13, she was sexually assaulted by a member of our church congregation. You can only imagine how this impacted her, and me as her father. To make things worse, this gentleman was well-liked in the ward and as things spiraled, people in the congregation began to take sides.

Over the next two years our family had to deal with the court system, the trauma from the initial assault, and the blowback from members of our ward. The church leaders didn't handle it in the best way, and since I was in the stake presidency at the time, I got to see an unvarnished view of everything. The man was convicted and sent to prison for seven years. It ruined his life and broke his family. But my family was breaking too. My daughter had been assaulted, our faith shaken, and we had become targets of anger in the one place where we should feel safe.

*"Love your enemies."*

I had faced school bullies who tried to degrade me because of my ethnicity; I had faced thoughtless teachers and racist systems, but I had been able to forgive and love.

This time?

How could I forgive a man, let alone *love* him, after he did something like this to my precious daughter?

I sat with this question for a while. I had to deal with the pain of his actions along with the frustrations of members of my faith siding with him because he was a gregarious guy. What could I do?

My mind began focusing on repentance, asking God for forgiveness of my sins. I needed to repent as much as anyone else did.

I needed the Atonement of Christ as much as my enemy. If I sought forgiveness from the people around me, and from my God, seeking the peace that comes from being clean, I could let go of my hate and resentment and learn to love. If I held onto that hate though, it would destroy me.

And so, I sought repentance for myself. As I felt forgiveness, I was able to begin to forgive the man who hurt my daughter. I wasn't the judge here. I had done what I could to protect other young women from him, and he had been convicted through those efforts and the efforts of others in the community. Whether he sought repentance didn't matter. If I was to receive forgiveness, I needed to forgive.

And I did.

I got on my knees and begged the Lord to take away my hate. I would give it to my Savior if God would take it away and replace it with a greater understanding of His love for all of us. It took time and effort, but eventually the peace of forgiveness spread through my heart and I was able to move on.

When we repent, our forgiveness for others expands. If we can't forgive though, then our repentance is not true. Our anger will fester, and our love will be tainted. It will become harder to love, not just the enemy you hate, but everyone. You can't pick and choose love and hate. They are nondirectional. When we hate someone, that hate infects every other relationship. The same is true for love, though. When we truly love, that love extends beyond us.

I would rather love than hate.

Do I love my enemy now?

Yes, as I constantly seek my own repentance and forgiveness. I can love him as a son of God who will be judged according to a perfect standard that I can't comprehend. All I know is that I want to be worthy of love, and thus I must give love to all. It doesn't change what he did, but it does change me, and that's enough.

In a non-religious sense, these principles are exactly the same. If you don't believe in God or Jesus Christ, talk of repentance has no meaning. But the nondirectional truth of love and hate is not a religious principle. If you want to live a full life where the people around you feel your love and safety, you must abandon hate. Hate cannot be a part of who you are. It will eat you alive.

Think about all the bad things you've done. Do you want those mistakes to be the only thing you're remembered for? Of course not! You want forgiveness for those things from the people you hurt. Think about that, and you'll start to feel your own need for forgiveness, even though it isn't from any God you believe in. You want the people in your life to forgive you, and when you feel they have forgiven your mistakes, you can begin to forgive those around you too.

Again, this is the hardest thing in the world. There are people in your life who may have done horrible things to you or people you care about. It's easy to hate them and wish them pain and anguish. But the more we cultivate those emotions, the more they destroy us. I don't want that man to do any more damage to me, or my daughter, than what he's already done. I would hate to think I gave him that type of power to destroy me.

I free myself through forgiveness and love. It's not easy, but it's a choice that will save me, and all of us, from emotional destruction.

## LOVE AND BUSINESS

"You're letting me go?"

I was sitting in my office at the clinic across from one of my employees. She looked disappointed and confused.

"Yes," I replied. "And you'll eventually understand, this is the best thing for everyone. It really is."

She certainly didn't see what I was doing at that moment as an act of love, but I did. She couldn't feel the energy of love because she only saw an uncertain future where she no longer had a job. I saw the energy of opportunity...as well as the energy of an employee who, despite months of additional training and numerous warnings, chose not to fulfill her duties to any satisfactory metric.

It was time to let her move on to another job better suited for her, and the positive energy that would come with that transition.

That energy would be real and carry real power.

That isn't simply my naïve way of seeing the world, either. Science backs the reality of energetic impact on the physical world.

I was recently reading a study that talked about how everything, including energy and information, is physical. All the data on the internet is actually electrical impulses that in fact have mass and weight to them, be it a tiny amount. If you took every gigabyte of information on the internet everywhere in the world, it would weigh about the same as a common strawberry.[7] Nothing heavy, mind you, but still having weight.

When thought about in these terms it's far easier to understand what I've been talking about with the energy of our actions actually impacting the people around us.

When we vibrate at the frequency of love, others truly feel the weight of our words and deeds. It's not some metaphysical mystery, but rather a true interaction of physical matter.

And that physical impact is noticeable, particularly in business.

Love in business is often overlooked because it's mistakenly seen as too soft, sentimental, or even inappropriate for professional environments. But in truth, when understood as care, respect, service, and sincere connection, love is one of the most powerful forces a

---

[7] https://www.wired.com/story/weight-of-the-internet/

business can harness.

At its core, love in business means treating others, be they employees, customers, or partners, with the same level of dignity and sincerity. People are drawn to businesses where they feel valued. That emotional connection breeds loyalty that no discount or flashy marketing campaign can replicate.

Creating products and verifying they are safe for consumers is an act of love, not just the law. We care about the people buying from us. *"I love myself, so I love my customers,"* right? Most people enter business to make money. They stay in business though because they care about what they're building and who they're building it for.

That's love in action.

Businesses that forget this may still make money, but they won't find the same meaning in their work, which then translates to less success and eventual burnout.

This extends to employees and workplaces as well. Companies driven by competition, ego, or fear often push their talent toward the door. But when love is present in the form of compassion, understanding, and shared purpose, teams stick together through challenges. Love fosters psychological safety. This leads to creativity, collaboration, and long-term success.

Now, having said this, sometimes love in business (and leadership) takes the form of letting people go so that the rest of a company can thrive. Not every job is a good fit for every person. That means sometimes terminating an employee is an act of love, even if they can't see it at that moment.

I've had this experience several times throughout my career. Normally I try to work with employees at my clinics to help turn them into the kinds of workers that expand a business. It doesn't always work out, unfortunately.

I had one employee who was trying hard, but never quite fit into the position. The longer she worked, the worse things became. Eventually I had to take her aside and let her go. I saw this as an act of love. I wasn't firing her because I didn't like her as a person or anything like that. The role didn't align with her strengths. It was clear she was struggling, and I was too. No leader enjoys delivering that kind of news. But I knew honesty was the most respectful, and ultimately, loving path forward

She of course was very unhappy with the situation.

"You're firing me!" she lamented. "I'm not going to have any money to pay my bills. What am I going to do? How can you do this to me?"

When we really love people, we want what's best for them. I honestly didn't know what type of job would be the best fit for her, or what would bring her true happiness and fulfillment, but I knew it wasn't working at the clinic. Keeping her in that role wasn't fair to her, or the team. The only reason she hadn't left yet was because she was worried about what would happen if she had to look for another job. It was all fear-based.

And to be honest, I had some fear too.

What would I look like if I fired her? Would I be seen as a brute who doesn't care what happens to people after they lose a job? Would I be a bad boss because I had failed to nurture her into a better employee?

You can see how all of these fears and emotions compete and conflict when talking about love in the workplace.

In the end, my love for her outweighed my need to feel good about myself.

She needed to be let go so the business could thrive, and so she could find a place that could bring her joy.

"You're not happy here," I said. "Your work shows that. If I keep you on, I won't be doing you, or the rest of the team any favors."

She left angrily.

If you've ever had to terminate an employee, you'll know exactly what I'm talking about here. Sometimes the most loving thing you can do is tell someone the truth they need to hear, even when it's uncomfortable.

And keeping someone in a position where they are consistently failing or unhappy can actually *harm* them. It robs them of the discomfort that triggers growth. And yes, discomfort is necessary for our progress, even though we long to be constantly comfortable. Few individuals end up doing amazing things if they are comfortable 24/7. It's our job as leaders to open doors to better paths, even if that means initiating a hard conversation. A loving leader doesn't enable mediocrity or misery.

Love means treating people like adults. If an employee has been given clear feedback, support, and fair opportunity to change, but chooses not to, it's respectful to acknowledge that choice and let them go. It honors their agency rather than dragging them along in a false relationship.

Once the team member is unencumbered by a job they really aren't suited for, most of the time they find something better. Many people who are terminated from a job later admit it was the best thing that ever happened to them. Why? Because it forced them to reevaluate and discover a path suited to their skill level and drive. A loving termination allows the employee to discover what's on the other side of that moment of struggle.

The key here is in the term '*loving termination.*' It can't be mean, like a lot of managers do. They put the employee down or let their anger and frustration get the better of them. You can't do that if you truly care about the employee. Yes, you need to be honest, but it can't feel like an attack.

I always give my employees chances before a termination. I am very clear about what is expected of them and what will happen if they don't elevate their performance. Once they've proven they won't do that, they are already expecting to get fired anyway.

And I do the same thing in my ecclesiastical callings. In the Church of Jesus Christ of Latter-day Saints, all callings are volunteer. If you're serving as an instructor for a Sunday school class, you were asked to do that calling by one of the leaders in the church and then you accepted it before taking the role. Obviously, not everyone serves with the same zeal, effort, or effectiveness.

When releasing a person from a call, I am always honest about why they are being released. Sometimes it's because they've held the calling for many years and it's simply time for a change. Other instances though, people have neglected their duty and done a bad job.

I'm not going to tell them they did great service when they didn't.

I'll say, "Brother, the reason you are being released is because you consistently don't show up to perform your calling. You're creating a burden for other people in their own service, and so we are releasing you from this position. I hope that when we call you for another service opportunity you will accept it with the understanding that this is sacred service, and our efforts are amplified by the Lord."

Some people might see that as being overly harsh. I see it as love in action. I give good people that moment of discomfort so they can progress toward better things.

The same is true in all our loving relationships. Love doesn't mean codling or avoiding difficult conversations. And these conversations shouldn't be avoided, even if they're with a sibling, a child, a spouse, a friend, or a colleague.

Love requires us to be brave.

And when we are, the energy of love touches the hearts of the people around us. I've had many experiences with bad employees who become great employees because they felt I had true love for them and cared about their progression. I've had far more people in my church accept a bit of honest correction and improve in their callings than I've had people get offended and walk away.

Love isn't a weakness in business.

It's clarity, courage, and compassion in action. It's the fuel that helps people grow, relationships deepen, and organizations thrive.

When we love God, love ourselves, and love others, we tap into the ultimate principle of success.

# CHAPTER 8

## FROM INSPIRATION TO IMPLEMENTATION

The garage door creaked as my brother lifted it open. Cool air blew in my face, contrasting against the heat of the afternoon sun.

"Here it is," he said, motioning toward the car parked among the scattered tools and greasy rags strewn everywhere. The car was in pretty good shape from what I could see. My brother had been working on the vehicle for a while. It had some wear and tear but overall looked like it would get the job done.

That was until my brother pointed at it and said, "It has some type of electrical problem. Nobody has been able to get the thing to work. You want it? It's yours, but it's worthless."

I looked at the car again. An electrical problem? That didn't seem like such a big deal. Surely, I could get it fixed. I wasn't going to pass up a free automobile.

At 17 years old, I knew how to work on a car. I had learned from local mechanics since I was a little kid. I would go into shops and ask if there were any odd jobs I could do, and after that, I would watch the technicians work on the vehicles.

I was confident I'd be able to get this car running again.

But it didn't turn out to be as easy as my young mind envisioned. I looked everything over myself and quickly concluded that, as my brother had said, it was some sort of electrical problem...I just couldn't figure out what the exact malfunction was. No matter what I did, the car would not start. Everything else seemed to be in perfect working order. I spent hours and hours taking things apart and putting them back together, but every time I turned that key, nothing happened. It was maddening!

Who could I turn to for help?

The Lord knew everything, right? Could I go to him for something as trivial as fixing a car? Could I seek inspiration for something like this?

Lucky for me, I had known since I was 10 years old the steps I needed to take if I wanted an answer from God. First, I would try and figure it out myself, then take it to other authorities who might know the answer, and then if none of that panned out, I could take it to the Lord himself and expect an answer.

After asking my brother who the best mechanic in town was, I took the vehicle to this man's office to check things out. He looked at the car, ran tests on everything and said, "Well, I can't figure it out. I know it's an electrical problem, but I don't know where it is. Take it to this other guy across town. He might be able to find the problem."

So, I took the car to mechanic Number 2. After checking everything himself and running a number of other tests, he shrugged his shoulders. "I can't figure it out either, man. I don't know where the problem is. I know you already took it to my competitor, and if he couldn't figure it out, and I can't figure it out, nobody's going to figure it out. Sorry."

Not exactly what I wanted to hear.

Even so, I knew I had one more thing I could do. I mean, I had access to the greatest mechanic in the universe, right?

I knelt down to pray. I told Him, "Hey, Heavenly Father, you already know I'm trying my best with this car. It has potential, you know, for me to drive and all that. But it's got this electrical problem. Nobody can figure it out! Maybe you can help me with this."

And that night, I had a dream. A voice said to me, "Do you see the car?"

I looked, and there was the car right in front of me. I said, "Yes, I see it."

"Do you see the four headlights?"

"Yes," I answered. "Two on the left and two on the right."

The voice continued. "The second headlight on the left. I want you to take it off and you will find the problem there."

I woke up, surprised by the dream. The Lord hadn't specifically told me how to fix the car, rather where I should look so I could fix it myself. I got up pretty early because I couldn't sleep after that. I ran and got a screwdriver and popped off the second headlight on the left. And there it was! A wire linking to the headlight was loose and touching the frame of the car. Such a simple thing, but every time a current ran through it, the body of the car would short it out, leading to an electrical problem for the entire system. I just put the wire back where it belonged, tightened it in place, and tried starting the car. For the first time since my brother had bought the vehicle, the engine started. It hummed perfectly as if there had never been a problem at all.

That moment of inspiration had given me the focus I'd needed to solve the problem. I first tried to find the answer myself, then I'd gone to experts for a solution, and when none of that worked, I turned to the Lord for guidance.

And He had given it, though not in the exact way I had expected.

# OUR NEED FOR INSPIRATION

We all have moments of inspiration in our lives. It's that flash of knowledge that we couldn't have gained on our own. Oftentimes it's a contradiction of the 'logical.' You are asked to do something that wouldn't be the normal thing to do in that circumstance. We suddenly know things that would have been impossible for us to know beforehand.

And if you're still in the mindset that intuition is merely coincidence, you're reading the wrong book. If I haven't proven to you by now (or at least nudged you toward the understanding) that inspiration is real and powerful, then I've failed in my mission with these words.

Inspiration is real.

Accept it; and accept that you can receive it just as regularly and powerfully as I have.

Inspiration emerges as a spiritual catalyst; a living energy that moves people toward higher versions of themselves. It's not simply motivation or encouragement. It's something deeper, more sacred. For some people, this is the power of the subconscious mind. If that's how you need to think about it, I don't have a problem with that. I of course see it through the spiritual lens, and so God gets the credit. Whatever it is, the end result is the same: we have knowledge or instruction we didn't have before.

And sometimes the instructions and thoughts you get don't make logical sense. Why would I have trusted a dream telling me to go look under one of the lights for the electrical problem? It isn't logical. None of the professionals did that. And yet, it proved to be the exact right course of action.

It takes courage to follow inspiration for that reason. And

oftentimes sacrifice too. Imagine telling someone you feel inspired to do something that on the surface seems strange or counterintuitive. It's easier not to follow the inspiration because you avoid any risk associated with the action. But if you trust in your intuition and yourself, you'll take that risk every day.

We must be vulnerable enough to know we don't have all the answers, and courageous enough to act. If we don't trust that we can receive inspiration, we'll never receive it. Just like respect and faith have an energetic frequency, so does inspiration. And it's often blocked by ego, fear, or control. Inspiration arrives when we let go of the need to be right and instead listen. The humble seeker will be given whispers of knowledge; from there it's their choice whether to act or not.

The answers I've received through inspiration have rarely been what I wanted them to be, or what I would have chosen for myself. I had originally tried to join the military after my proselyting mission but had been disqualified because of my hearing. That door was shut...or so I thought. As I sat in one of my college classes, I heard that familiar voice in my head say, "It's time to go into the military." I was confused of course because I had already tried to get into the armed services and had been rejected.

But I knew better than to argue with the Spirit!

So, I enlisted in the Air Force...and got rejected. Then the Marines, the Navy, all of them disqualified me because of my hearing. Finally, I tried the Army. They reached back out and said, "You're licensed as a vocational nurse. That's good. We can take you." So, I got in.

If I hadn't followed that inspiration, I never would have met my wife, who was a woman I had been praying to meet since I was 10 years old. It was also while I was in the military that I was able to expand my medical skills and prepare for the path the Lord had in store for me to serve my fellow men. During Operation: Desert Storm, I was assigned to a unit that provided medical care and was deployed as a medic. We were seeing 80 to 90 patients per day.

I had courage to listen and act on something I thought was crazy. But in truth, was that whispering any more or less impactful than those I had already received? Wasn't going and hiding a gun a strange thought to act on? Wasn't popping off a headlight and finding the cause of an entire electrical system failure? Joining the military at that exact moment was the impetus for everything that came after.

God uses inspiration to guide us. If we follow that softly spoken thought, we will reach heights we never dreamed of.

## RECEIVING INSPIRATION

Inspiration involves all of the principles we've covered so far. If you want communication from a higher source, be it God or the universe, all of the ethics are involved. They must be implemented in concrete ways to help you align with the will of the Divine.

Let's delve into what that looks like.

Start with Obedience. Apply that in your life by looking at ways you are currently being disobedient. Are you following the laws of the road when you drive? What about small things like using your blinker? Are you being obedient to the laws that irritate you, or that you may disagree with? Are you paying your taxes?

Find where you can improve your obedience and simply tell yourself you are going to obey those things at a higher level. It may sound tedious, but if you want true inspiration, you need to shore up your actions first.

Are you being honest in business and personal relationships, or are you just saying what people want to hear because that's how you get an advantage? You're either honest or dishonest. If you're not telling the truth, you're being deceitful. You need to decide today what type of person you're going to be.

When implementing respect, you first need to listen to what people actually want. Are you paying attention to how they *want* to be treated? Are you then respecting them in that way?

Too often we treat people disrespectfully because they are different from us and we think them strange or weird. How we perceive them doesn't matter, though. If we love everyone then we respect everyone. Here's a simple personal example. I was once meeting a pharmaceutical rep for lunch on my birthday. I specifically asked them not to have anyone sing to me at the table because I absolutely do not like it.

Did they listen?

Nope.

After the awkward song I told them they did not respect me as a person. They were taken aback by this, but I told them they had not even listened to my basic request from ten minutes before. They may have loved being sung to for their birthday, but I did not, and I made sure to tell them that. What *they* wanted in that situation became more important than what *I* wanted. And if I had said nothing, it would have been disrespectful to them because I wouldn't have shared important information about the circumstance and why I was choosing not to do business with them.

Show respect first by listening and following through.

Self-belief is huge when it comes to inspiration. I wasn't the smartest kid growing up, nor the one with the most advantages, but I learned that if I put in the effort, and I believed that I could do it, then I could accomplish anything.

That's where my self-belief started.

I still say the same thing today: I can accomplish anything I want, and if it's the will of the Lord to do more, I can do that too. With that kind of belief, you open the doors to divine communication. You have no doubt in yourself, which means you have no doubt in the Lord.

Finally, faith and love follow the same pattern. You practice those principles while you're developing them. You have faith that you can receive heavenly ideas, and you act on that faith. You love yourself enough to realize you are worthy of divine communication.

We start at the level that we're at.

As long as we're willing to sacrifice the time and effort needed to foster our mindset, inspiration will come. All of this is tied together by energy. If we're willing to accept that, we'll commit ourselves to seeking and implementing inspiration when it comes.

But how do we get into that space of inspiration, and how do we then implement it in a way that leads to powerful results? After my experience as a 10-year-old, I made a commitment to myself that I would seek inspiration from then on in any circumstance where I needed guidance.

I committed to myself and to the Lord.

Depending on your religious beliefs, you may not make a commitment to a Father in Heaven, but you must still make a commitment to yourself and to the people around you.

Once we commit, and are honest about that commitment to ourselves, we can begin to receive. First trust (believe) something is possible, then take the action, and finally receive the reward. Just like with my experience with the car, I first tried to fix it myself, then I went to a couple mechanics, and finally I trusted in God to help me. I went through the process first and eventually received my answer. Through this method we're learning patience, we're learning discipline, we're learning the principles that really refine us.

So much of this is mindset, and that goes double for inspiration. If we have a mindset of belief in God, or ourselves at the very least, answers can be ours.

# THE PROCESS WORKS

We don't need inspiration in every circumstance. That's one of the reasons we go through the process first of trying to find the answer ourselves and then seeking guidance from mentors. Sometimes after those first two steps, we'll no longer need the inspiration.

If I want to succeed in business, I can't simply ask God to give me success. When I learn about my industry, seek counsel from people who have succeeded in that business, and put in the effort, I often find the answers myself. We seek inspiration for the things that can't be known, or the problems that can't be solved after having gone through the previous steps.

Next, we need to think about our environment when seeking inspiration. It's not just *what* you're asking for, but *how* and *where* you're asking for it. Are you in a place where your mind is open to receive inspiration? Aside from the obvious religious connotations here of seeking inspiration in sacred spaces, think about it in terms of clarity of mind.

Will your mind be clear if you are in a chaotic place?

Are noises and other stimuli competing for your attention?

That's why so many people pray at the end of the night in the quiet of their bedrooms away from the rest of the world. Yes, inspiration can come in the most unexpected times and places, but if we are actively seeking it, thoughts of where and when become important.

So, find a place where your mind can be quiet and focused. Meditate or pray, whichever is your form of seeking counsel from a higher power. If you have done the work up to this point to try and solve the problem yourself, you know you can trust that an answer will be received.

This is the hardest part, because you need to control your mind and your thoughts. You need to discipline yourself to remain focused. What you concentrate on will manifest, so if your mind is cluttered with negative thoughts or images, inspiration will be slow to arrive.

From there, you need to listen.

Inspiration may come quickly or take time. There's no rule book for this sort of thing. After praying for answers regarding the car, I had a dream that very night. On my mission when my companion and I were seeking guidance on where to go to find people ready to hear the Gospel of Jesus Christ, it took six hours of praying and incremental steps of inspiration until I saw in my mind that we needed to go to Cherry Street.

I can't tell you what will happen.

All of this is personal and should be pursued from a personal space. But, if you have implemented the six principles in your life, you can expect to receive inspiration. One thing follows another. You do the work, and the Lord will always make sure you are guided.

## ACTION IS THE KEY INGREDIENT

If you think about it, you are given moments of inspiration all the time. You think, out of nowhere, about contacting someone you haven't spoken to in a long time. You wake up one morning and decide to drive to work a different way than usual.

These may sound like random thoughts, but when we follow them, the results are always positive.

There is nothing random about it.

When we receive a prompting, idea, or spark, we're being handed divine momentum. If we sit on it, ignore it, or rationalize it away, we aren't just missing an opportunity, we're sending a message that we weren't ready to steward that insight.

And sometimes that insight is small and fleeting.

One day I was looking through my planner while on my mission. I had calendars and lists of appointments that went back several months, so I needed to do a bit of spring cleaning. While clearing out pages that no longer needed to be taking up space, I saw that one of them had the name of a family that we had taught about Jesus written on it. They were interested in learning more, but they lived outside of our area. I knew there were no missionaries near where they lived, but they weren't near us either, so there wasn't much I could do. I was getting ready to tear it out and toss it in the trash with the other papers when the Spirit whispered to me, *"Don't throw it away, save it!"*

No further instruction followed.

This didn't make any sense to me. Why would I keep that family name? We had already taught them. They were out of our area. It wasn't like we were going to go teach them again.

But I listened to that little bit of inspiration, and I kept the page in my planner. It was with me every day for weeks. Then one morning the phone in our apartment rang.

It was the president of the entire mission!

"Elder Mendez," the president said. "I have been pondering some questions, and I felt like you were the right missionary for me to call."

Now I was intrigued...and a little nervous.

"Okay, President," I said. "You really need my help answering a question?"

"Yes, Elder Mendez. We are getting two new missionaries, and I don't know where to send them to teach. I want them to be able to teach some great people, but I'm stumped. Again, I felt prompted to ask you. What are your thoughts? What do you recommend?"

Immediately my mind went to the name of the family in my planner. That family was waiting to be taught the gospel. There were no missionaries in the area where this family lived. I knew at that moment that these two new missionaries could open up that area, and this family would accept Jesus Christ and be baptized.

I pulled the page from the planner and held it in front of my eyes.

"I know where you can send those missionaries, and I have a family that's waiting to be baptized," I told the president. "They're just outside our area and we've talked with them a few times. Here's the name, the address, and the phone number."

The mission president opened a new teaching area on the edge of our own based on my recommendations. And you know what? That family was baptized two weeks later by these two new missionaries.

Imagine if I had thrown that paper away as I had intended. It made no logical sense for me to keep it. But by listening to that strange thought, miracles occurred.

If you listen to your feelings, you will always be doing the right thing. When the time comes, you'll know what to do next. That's the big blessing of following your intuition because you're not doing it on your own. When you make decisions alone, you don't have that energy or the spirit to give you guidance and power. But when you do have these principles of faith, respect, and inspiration, you're not alone. And everybody around you will feel it. They'll start to make decisions based on their feelings too, and the energy will build.

When you act on inspiration, even if it doesn't yield immediate success, it keeps you spiritually aligned. It trains your intuition. It protects you from wasting time chasing the wrong things. Inspired action clarifies your purpose in a way that nothing else can. When you act on inspiration, especially when it's inconvenient, uncomfortable, or seems small, you signal to God (and to yourself): "I'm ready. I'm listening. I'm trustworthy."

If you believe those things, inspiration will flow. You'll be a conduit to help others, and by helping others, you'll always have everything you need and more.

At the end of the day, inspiration isn't just a gift, it's a test. Unacted inspiration doesn't just die; it fades your ability to receive more. You lose confidence in yourself. You dull your spiritual senses. Like a muscle unused, your receptivity atrophies.

Stay receptive. Stay focused. Open your mind and heart. From there, the windows of heaven will open, and you will enjoy a new level of communication.

It's worked for me, and it will work for you too.

# CHAPTER 9

## FULL CIRCLE: PROGRESSION AND CHANGE

I woke up at 3am in excruciating pain. Staring at the dark ceiling, sweat accumulated on my forehead and upper lip. I had felt mild discomfort in my side as I'd gone to bed, but I thought it was just indigestion. Now? The pain had woken me up and threatened to send me into a spasm.

What could be wrong? My side hurt, my back hurt. It was pain unlike anything I'd ever felt before. I was only 36 years old, and in good shape. Maybe if I walked around a bit, I could ease the agony.

As I stood though, my legs gave out.

I collapsed and started rolling around on the floor.

I thought for a moment the pain would kill me, or at the very least, leave me unconscious.

A thought came to my mind, "Please Heavenly Father, let me go unconscious so I don't have to feel this torture!"

My wife took me to the hospital immediately. We rushed into

the ER. The doctors knew right away what it was. I hadn't had much experience with kidney stones up to that point, but I knew how excruciating they could be for patients. Now I had personal experience with them. The doctors gave me an injection, and I waited it out.

That was my first kidney stone.

Definitely not my last.

After I continued to develop stones regularly, my colleagues discovered that I was born with a horseshoe-shaped kidney, meaning my kidneys are stuck together. Particles pass through like in a normal kidney, but in a sort of loop pattern. Instead of going straight down into the bladder, waste accumulates in the bottom section of the kidney, which then forms into stones on a regular basis. Over the past 15 years I've passed kidney stones almost weekly. I passed a stone two days ago as of this writing.

Now, some people would say this is a bad thing, or a negative thing. I'm dealing with kidney stones all the time, and that must be terrible.

Well, it is, and it isn't.

You see, part of our mortal existence here on Earth involves pain and discomfort, weakness and illness. The interesting thing is that as we go through these times of hardship, we're strengthened so we can handle them. I give credit to God, of course. He gives me strength. He lightens my burdens so I can carry them.

Over the years of passing stones, my ability to cope with the pain has increased to the point that when I feel one coming on, I just shrug and wait it out, knowing it will pass...literally. The pain no longer disrupts my life or causes me to roll around on the floor. I feel it, but it's no big deal. Sometimes when it hurts more than normal, I take a simple Tylenol, and I'm fine.

My pain tolerance didn't improve overnight. It was earned, stone by stone, until what once dropped me to the floor now barely slows me down.

## SPIRITUAL TRIALS

Like physical trials, spiritual trials stretch us and prepare us for the next stage of growth, both in this life and the next. Everything in life follows this same pattern. Throughout this book we've talked about principles that allow each of us to reach our full potential. They expand our capacity and allow us to reach heights undreamed of before.

This is a probationary life. Whatever skills, knowledge, or experience we gain is taken with us once we pass through death. And after that, we continue to progress. That's why it's called Eternal Progression.

The Lord taught me that we can progress in the next life, but at a slower pace than we can here. Right now, we're moldable like clay. Once we go through the fire of death, change becomes much more difficult. For some people it will take a thousand years to progress to a point that allows them to reach their full potential. For others, most of the work will be done here in mortality, allowing them to progress incredibly quickly in the next life. Either way, it all comes down to the principles of obedience, honesty, self-belief, faith, respect, and love.

It's up to you how far you want to progress.

There's no limit.

And let me tell you, it's easier to progress when you have someone by your side progressing with you. I haven't talked much about my wife in this book beyond how we met (and the fact that she rushed me to the hospital that first time I had kidney stones), but let me tell you, I would not have progressed as far as I have without her by my side. If you're single, that's fine, but just know that true progression happens with a partner challenging you and helping support the load.

I'm a big proponent of marriage and family. Having a spouse and children pushes you toward progression pretty much constantly. There's no escaping it.

I love my wife. She has been my companion and sounding board for many decades. We've gone through all the standard marriage trials and come out the other side stronger. We've progressed together. She has shouldered the same stresses that I have when it comes to military service, medical training, the challenges of building a franchise of clinics and having to let them go because of the actions of a business partner. And she was with me as we rebuilt and forged ahead at every turn. Progression is possible alone, but it's amplified with a partner. Side by side, you don't just grow; you multiply.

And having kids?

That is the ultimate progression profession. Here you have little humans that think and feel for themselves, trying to emulate you and surpass you all at the same time. It's a tornado of emotion and chaos. You can't help but progress in those circumstances. If I had a dollar for every time I prayed for patience regarding one of my children, I could have retired a decade ago. And the more I prayed for patience, the more opportunities I received to be patient. My kids helped me become a better person. I'm just glad my shortcomings as a father didn't mess them up too badly.

The point I'm making here is that we are in mortality to progress, and we progress because of other people.

The Lord is always there cheering us on, and He is closer than you might think.

## THE LIGHT OF CHRIST

When the Lord spoke to me when I was 10 years old, He said,

"All My Children here on Earth have been given the Light of Christ."

"What is that?" I asked.

"It is a connection, directly to me. You can never lose that connection. It might not work very well because of your actions, but you never lose it. If you're not worthy, my voice will be more difficult to hear. But if you're worthy, and you have the desire to speak with me and do what's right, then that connection, that door, will open up and you have a direct link with me. Every single child here, every single person on the earth, has the same privileges and rights that you have right now speaking to me, Ricardo. Anyone can speak to me directly like you are, if they so desire, but because the things of the world and other distractions get in the way, it causes them to forget that I am who I am, and that they are who they are: Children of God. And here I am, waiting for them whenever they want to speak to me."

This is the most profound statement I've ever heard. It changed my life more than anything God said that terrifying and enlightening night. I suddenly knew God was there for me – and not just for me, but for everyone.

All of us have the right to speak to our Father in Heaven and expect a response. A real response. He is there at all times. If we knock at the door, it will be opened.

That doesn't mean it will always be quick or effortless. I prayed from the day my mother first told me God answers prayers, and it took years before I had my initial communication. I showed faith and endurance – and finally, I received His message.

Just because it doesn't happen immediately doesn't mean we should give up. When we ask for great things, sometimes the Lord requires great effort.

I'm not some anomaly that Heavenly Father decided to reach out to. I'm nobody. And yet God saw fit to answer my prayer in a very direct and powerful manner. You can receive the same privilege and benefits. You can! I know it. I may be a bit more sensitive to it, but most of that has been learned by listening and acting.

It requires work.

It requires dedication.

It requires the understanding that we must put ourselves in alignment with Him, not the other way around.

Most of us, even those who are religious, wait for the commanding presence of the Spirit of God to shout at us what to do, instead of learning to walk alongside it.

As we act obediently, respond honestly, believe in ourselves and our abilities, have faith in God and other people, respect the law and those who uphold it, and love our fellow men and women with the same love we claim to feel for God, our communication with the celestial will flourish.

And from there, our progression is infinite.

# THE THREE PHASES OF LIFE

Life is made up of three phases of progression. This realization came to me many years ago, but as I've aged, becoming a grandparent and gray-haired professional, it has been reinforced again and again. The three phases are The Beginning Phase, The Failure Phase, and The Problem Phase. Each of these phases is applicable in personal pursuits, business, family, and spiritual belief. We'll hit them from all those angles.

**The Beginning Phase**

The Beginning Phase is the one that everyone goes through. It starts at birth and continues as we grow and learn. It's in this Beginning Phase where we decide, as an individual, how much we want to grow, how fast, and how much experience we want to get. Everyone progresses in different ways. We get to choose our own progression path. This is when we're deciding what kind of person we want to be. Are we honest? Are we hardworking? Are we loving? Once those choices are made during the Beginning Phase of life, they are hard to change later. When we're kids, we are so malleable. As we grow, we harden. I think you'll find that so many of your habits, both good and bad, were formed during childhood.

### The Failure Phase

The second phase, or Failure Phase, can also be called the Repentance Phase if you look at things through a more spiritual lens, as I do. The Failure Phase is when you start to mature, test your limits, and trip over obstacles you didn't realize were in your way. Think of it like building a business. You know accounting is required, but you don't know accounting. You know marketing is going to be required, but you know nothing about marketing. Budgeting is required but you know nothing about budgeting. Finally, you know that hard work is required as well.

If you choose not to learn those things or fail to show up when you need to work, your business is likely to fail.

This type of failure has more to do with experience...or a lack thereof. These are things you should have known from the very beginning of whatever endeavor you're pursuing, be it business or family. You simply lacked the experience to appreciate how badly you needed to know them, or how to make them work together for your benefit.

Now, I hate to break it to you if no one has told you this before, but you're going to fail.

That's a good thing.

The more you fail, the more experience you gain, which means you have more knowledge, which makes you less likely to fail the next time. Most things you try at first in business won't work, and that's okay. Each misstep gets you closer to what does.

It's the same thing in spiritual and family matters as it is with business. We know what we're supposed to do, but we're not doing it. We're failing to keep the commandments, we're failing to go to church, we're failing to serve, we're failing to pay our taxes, we're failing to listen to our children.

So, that's what the Failure Phase means. You're learning and hopefully applying your knowledge to make things better for yourself and the people around you. You mess up, learn from it, and don't do it again.

Like I said, in the Spiritual World, we call it repentance. Right now, you're in the Repentance Phase. You still have a chance to make things better. No failure is permanent until you stop trying. As long as you're putting out the effort to learn what you need to learn, work as hard as you need to work, and believe you can make amazing things happen, then you're going to succeed. At that point you can call it the Success Phase if you want, but I like Failure Phase better because I don't see failure as a negative thing. I see it as the ultimate teacher and mentor. Failure is your greatest educator. Accept it, learn fast, and move forward even faster.

## The Problem Phase

You can end here on the Failure Phase and continue on an upward trend for the rest of your existence, but if you're not willing to do the work because you don't have the faith and you don't believe, then you're going to progress (or regress) to the third phase, which is the Problem Phase. In the spiritual world, this is called the 'Now-You're-Under-the-Judgment-of-God' phase. You had a chance to repent, to change, to improve, but you didn't take it. Now you're in the judgment phase. You have no choices left, and you're going to get whatever is coming to you in judgment.

When you're in the Problem Phase in business, it's already too late. You didn't pay your taxes. Now the government's going to get you. You were dishonest in your dealings. You might go to jail now. You failed to adapt or learn what you needed about your business. You're going to have to close it down.

When you're in the problem phase, you are no longer in control. You're in the hands of God on the spiritual side, and you're in the hands of whoever is going to control you on the business side, be it the government, your partner, or the general public. There is now nothing you can do. That's a pretty big problem.

The Problem Phase is where forward motion stops and consequences take over. It's not punishment, but the natural result of unlearned lessons and ignored growth.

If you're paying attention, the phase you want to be in is the Failure Phase. This is where all of your choices and growth are in front of you. Making a mistake and failing is not the end, but the beginning. You fail, figure out what you did wrong, and find somewhere else to fail.

Failure is a great place to be.

## THE ENERGY OF CHANGE

As a kid, I would get angry when authorities would treat me or others unfairly. That rage could be explosive and hard to control. Elements of that young personality stick with me to this day, but I've progressed enough to understand there is room for change.

People can in fact become more than they are at this moment. I've seen it. I've lived it.

As a missionary, one day my companion and I stopped and knocked at the door of a local home. They were our neighbors, right next door. A woman in her 50s answered, and she was not particularly happy to see us. She listened as we taught for a little while, and then she threw us out of her house. This wasn't a 'Would you please leave?' sort of situation. This was anger and shouts and mean personal taunts screamed in our direction. We got out of there and decided we would never go back.

Weeks later while we were at church on Sunday, a member of our congregation stopped me and said, "Elder Mendez, I feel the Spirit whispering for me to tell you my story." He then went on to relate how as a youth he had suffered carbon monoxide poisoning, and the doctors thought he would be a vegetable for the rest of his life. He recovered, but it was incredibly difficult. During his recovery he found a book on origami that featured a little bird that could flap its wings. This brother pushed himself to be able to fold the paper in the right way to make that bird. It became his own personal goal, and when he accomplished it, it was an enormous triumph that taught him he could do anything.

He also shared how years later he had gotten his foot stuck in the railroad tracks and his dog had pulled him out before a train hit him. The dog had been hit and killed while freeing him at the last second, giving his life for his owner.

"I don't know why I felt like sharing these stories, but I wanted to follow the prompting of the Spirit."

The next day as we were leaving our apartment, I received my own spiritual prompting.

*"Go and share the story of the paper bird that flaps its wings with your neighbor."*

*"But she threw us out of her house last time,"* I said to myself. *"She was really mean."*

*"Share the story of the paper bird that flaps its wings with her; everything the brother told you in church. She will listen, and progress because of it."*

So, I listened.

The woman answered the door. An angry sneer contorted her face. "I thought I told you to get out of here and never come back!" she barked.

"You did," I said. "But the Spirit of God told me you needed to hear the story of the paper bird that flaps his wings and to bear my testimony. After that, we can leave if you want."

This caught her off-guard. She let us in. From there, I told her the story the brother from church had shared, all the way to his dog sacrificing himself to save him from the train. I concluded by sharing my testimony of God.

By the end, she was crying.

After that, we became great friends. She was like an older sister to me. Her aging mother lived with her as well, and she became like a second mother. She was very old, in her late 80's, and she grew to love us as well.

It turned out our neighbor had a lot of anger inside of her. Like me when I was a little boy, that anger would boil out of her in fits of rage. Once she realized that, she began to progress toward a more peaceful existence. It took effort as she applied eternal principles of success to her life, but the energy of those actions helped to bring her closer to the person she wanted to be.

"I won't be throwing anyone out of my house again," she beamed one day after one of our visits.

I had changed from that angry person...and so had she.

When I was leaving my mission to come home, she actually asked if I would write to the family and keep in contact. I had made a point of not promising that to anyone, since I wasn't good with language and didn't like writing letters.

"But Mama will miss you so," she said. "She wants to hear from you for the rest of her life."

I thought about it for a second. Mama was in her late 80's. She could die at any time. I'd have to write letters for a year; two at most.

"Alright," I replied. "I'll write to your family until Mom passes away. Deal?" I gave her my word.

"Deal!"

I ended up writing to that family until Mama died…15 years later.

I progressed in my ability to write letters; I can tell you that!

And that family progressed toward the life they wanted to live, simply by giving away their anger, and applying eternal principles to their own lives.

They had changed.

People *can* change!

*You* can change!

The application of the principles in this book requires self-discipline, pure and simple. Like everything we've discussed, it must first start with you. Respect yourself and you'll progress toward respecting others. Be honest with yourself and you'll find being honest with the people around you an easy and natural action.

We start with ourselves and then feel the desire to give others the same courtesy.

Think about it this way: when we're young, we're selfish. No one else matters. As we grow, we begin to see how our actions affect the people in our lives. As we mature, truly mature, we realize that worrying about ourselves serves no purpose. When we concentrate on serving other people, we end up getting everything we want.

That's the kind of progression I'm talking about. Start with yourself and then mature toward doing all that good for other people. Learn to master your own thoughts and actions and then become an example for others to follow.

And when you do that, the energy that flows from your every

action becomes a power that amplifies each deed. We've talked a lot about the energy of each principle. Now imagine the energy of all of them together, helping you progress toward eternal perfection. Imagine the power of your example as you touch the lives of others, inviting them to partake of that energy and magnify it in their own lives.

This is true joy and true freedom.

And so, it's time to make a choice. Who are you going to become? What impact are you going to have? God loves you no matter what you do. He is merciful no matter who you are. He wants you to pass through the Failure Phase again and again, learning, repenting, and growing. But you have to choose to do it. You have to choose to be faithful, respectful, obedient, and all the other principles.

You have to *choose* success.

You have to *choose* to change.

And change doesn't need to take months, years, or decades. Change can happen quickly and last forever.

My entire life is a testimony of those ideals. I keep trying to improve because I'm far from being a perfect man. The more I try, the better I become; more perfect, action by action. When you live your life in this way, you're becoming closer to perfection.

And that's what the Lord wants.

He wants us to continually try to become better, to do better. We'll never make it to perfection in this life, but He wants us to have the desire to progress and apply these values. You'll see a change in your life. You'll feel an energy within yourself, and you'll have more of a connection with the people who have that same energy. You'll start seeing people differently, feeling their energy differently, loving them differently, respecting them differently. And if you continue to improve, it just opens up opportunities in everything you do. You'll find greater success in family, business, and your personal pursuits. And on top of that, you'll inspire others to do the same.

The Lord wants us to work together and help each other progress. We can't progress by ourselves. We need each other.

So, the question remains: What are you willing to do?

Are you willing to change?

Are you willing to progress?

Every day we must ask ourselves those questions and make the decision to act. Luckily, we're not alone. We have support systems in our families, jobs, and friendships. We also have Christ at our side if we choose to welcome Him into our circle. We can go with Him or without Him. I can tell you which one of those I would prefer, but I'll let you make the choice yourself. Just know that Jesus Christ lives. I have no doubt about that.

You get to decide who you will be.

I make the choice every day to be obedient, honest, respectful, faithful, and to believe in myself. In doing so, I have created a life that includes everything I ever wanted.

Now, I want that for you too.

God told me during our first conversation that we all have the potential in us for success and progression in this mortal life and in the eternal life afterward. It is up to us to choose how much success or progress we want for the rest of our existence.

Make the choice.

Not because it's easy, but because you honestly want to succeed.

Progress is waiting.

So is everything you were born to become.

Success is within you!

Contact Ricardo about speaking to your business or congregation at:

**www.successwithinus.com**

# ABOUT THE AUTHOR

Army veteran Ricardo Mendez is a lover of learning. Certified as a Physician Assistant from Stanford University, along with having certifications as a paralegal and computer technician, Ricardo has accumulated over 700 university credit hours during his entrepreneurial journey. As the owner of ten medical clinics, Ricardo has treated and improved the lives of thousands of people in his community. He continues to serve in his church and local congregation in Brownsville, Texas, where he lives with his wife, Leticia. Ricardo and Leticia have four children, and four grandchildren.

www.ingramcontent.com/pod-product-compliance
Lightning Source LLC
LaVergne TN
LVHW010927110826
845149LV00013B/2505
* 9 7 9 8 9 9 4 5 6 5 7 0 4 *